Chatterbox

ENGLISH AS A SECOND LANGUAGE

Gillian Baxter
Jonathan Munro Jones
Hélène Bibeau

THIRD CYCLE, ELEMENTARY

ACTIVITY BOOK 2

ERPI
ÉDITIONS DU RENOUVEAU PÉDAGOGIQUE INC.

5757, RUE CYPIHOT
SAINT-LAURENT (QUÉBEC)
H4S 1R3

TÉLÉPHONE : (514) 334-2690
TÉLÉCOPIEUR : (514) 334-4720
COURRIEL : erpidlm@erpi.com

Project editor
Jocelyne Lauzière

Cover and book design
Tandem Conception et Infographie inc.

Illustrations
Danielle Bélanger: pages 1-8, 12-18, 31-48, 58-70, 77-90, 98-114, 118-128
Jocelyne Bouchard: pages 19-30, 71-76
Irina Georgeta Pusztai: pages 49-57, 91-97
Danièla Zékina: pages 9, 11, 115

Dépôt légal : 2e trimestre 2003
Bibliothèque nationale du Québec
National Library of Canada
Imprimé au Canada

ISBN 2-7613-1364-X
234567890 HLN 0987654
10550 ABCD OF10

Contents

Message to the Teacher

This full-colour Activity Book accompanies Student's Book 2 of the Chatterbox series for the third cycle. It replaces most of the reproducible handouts provided in the Teacher's Guide, thus relieving teachers of the time-consuming task of making photocopies. All instructions are written in clear, simple language, and the number of pictograms has been kept to a minimum to avoid confusion.

Activity Book 2 provides material to accompany the warm-up, the activities and the wrap-up of each unit of Student's Book 2. The Activity Book also contains one or more extension activities in each unit that can be used for remediation or enrichment, in class or at home. In addition, each unit ends with one and sometimes two extra activities that can be used for a variety of purposes.

Pictograms

This indicates the corresponding page in the Student's Book.

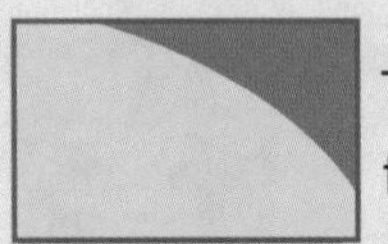

This section contains a questionnaire for student self-evaluation.

We hope you enjoy using *Chatterbox* and wish you a successful school year.

Chers parents,

Le but du cours d'anglais au primaire est de permettre aux enfants d'acquérir une connaissance fonctionnelle de la langue seconde. Ainsi, dès le premier jour de classe, votre enfant commencera à acquérir le vocabulaire de base et les stratégies d'apprentissage qui lui permettront d'échanger avec ses camarades de classe en anglais. Durant l'année scolaire, votre enfant sera appelé à participer à diverses activités qui visent surtout à développer la communication orale.

Le présent cahier soutient et renforce les activités du manuel de l'élève; il propose également des activités d'enrichissement en lien avec les thèmes abordés en classe. À la fin de chaque activité, de même qu'à la fin de chaque unité, votre enfant aura l'occasion de faire le point sur ses apprentissages à l'aide d'un questionnaire d'auto-évaluation. Nous vous encourageons à consulter régulièrement ces pistes d'évaluation afin de suivre le cheminement de votre enfant.

L'enseignante ou l'enseignant de votre enfant vous proposera des moyens pour poursuivre et consolider l'apprentissage de l'anglais à la maison. Parmi ces moyens, il y a en un qui nous semble plus important que les autres. Ce moyen, c'est de valoriser les efforts de votre enfant dans la langue seconde. L'importance que votre enfant accordera à l'apprentissage de l'anglais dépendra dans une large mesure de l'importance que vous y accorderez.

Recevez, chers parents, nos meilleures salutations.

Les auteurs de *Chatterbox*,

Gillian Baxter

Jonathan Munro Jones

Hélène Bibeau

All about Me!

Name:

Age:

Group:

Glue your photo here.

Favourite animal:

Favourite book:

Favourite cartoon character:

Favourite colour:

Favourite game:

Favourite meal:

Favourite pastime:

Favourite snack:

Favourite treat:

Favourite TV program:

Favourite Web site:

Unit 1

Learning Tools

Warm-up

SB 4

► Write down the first letter of each hidden word.

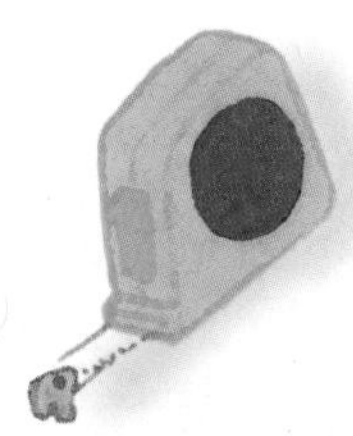     

► Unscramble the letters to find the mystery word. ______________________

- I found all the hidden words. Yes ☐ No ☐
- I found the mystery word with ☐ or without ☐ help.

Activity 1 Nonsense

► Decode the message.

babble = ______________________

blah = ______________________

blip = ______________________

- I decoded the words.
  All of them ☐ Most of them ☐ Some of them ☐ None of them ☐
- This activity was fun. Yes ☐ No ☐

Talk about a Riddle

- Write down the clues.
- Use the clues to solve the riddle.

Our Words				Our Solution

- I used Chatterbox 3 for help. Yes ☐ No ☐
- I worked quietly. Yes ☐ No ☐

Circle Talk

► **Make a list of the words you guessed.**

My Guess	Solution

- **I spoke English.**
  Always ☐ Most of the time ☐ Some of the time ☐ Never ☐
- **I guessed _______ words with my team.**

Tons of Tongue Twisters

SB 8

► **Make a list of the participants in the Tongue-Twister Tournament.**

► **Circle their ratings.**

Tongue Twisters	Participants	Rating*
She sells seashells by the seashore.		1 2 3
		1 2 3
		1 2 3
		1 2 3
A big black bug bit a big black bear.		1 2 3
		1 2 3
		1 2 3
		1 2 3
How much wood would a wood-chuck chuck, if a woodchuck could chuck wood?		1 2 3
		1 2 3
		1 2 3
		1 2 3
Peter Piper picked a pail of pickled peppers.		1 2 3
		1 2 3
		1 2 3
		1 2 3
If two witches were watching two watches, which witch would watch which watch?		1 2 3
		1 2 3
		1 2 3
		1 2 3
Happy Henry has hundreds of hens.		1 2 3
		1 2 3
		1 2 3
		1 2 3

* Ratings: 1 = Great! 2 = O.K. 3 = Try again.

- **I used Chatterbox 7 for help.** Yes ☐ No ☐
- **This activity was:**
  Very easy ☐ Easy ☐ Difficult ☐ Very difficult ☐

Extension Activity

More Tongue Twisters

► **Practise these tongue twisters.**

The hat she has on her head is heavy.

I scream, you scream,
we all scream for ice cream.

Three tin thimbles are under
three thin tables.

We shall surely see the sun shine soon.

Glue your tools in the toolbox.

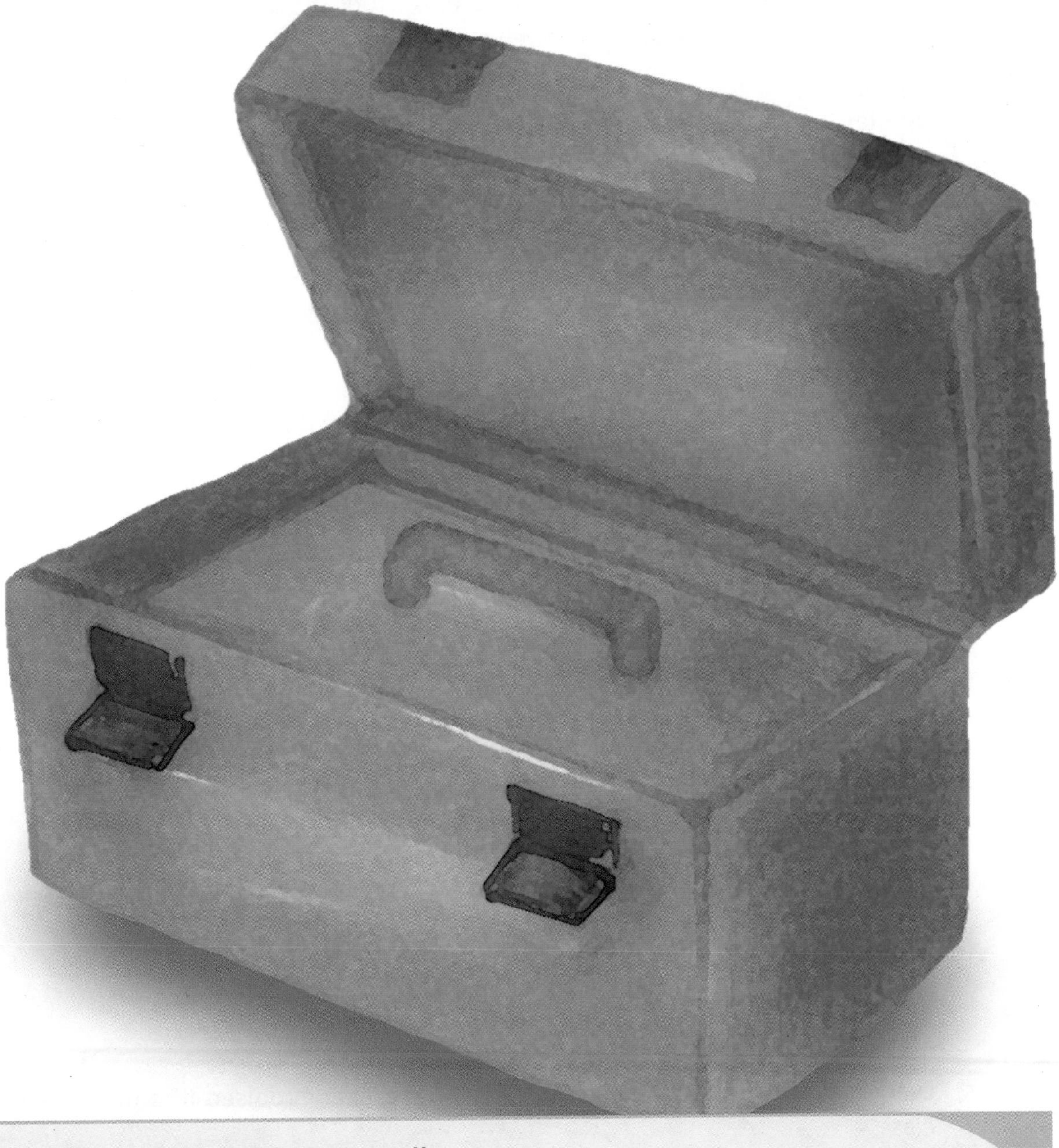

- I put _______ tools in my toolbox.
- I am satisfied with my work.
  Extremely ☐ Very ☐ Not very ☐ Not at all ☐

What Is It?

► **Guess what the strange words mean.**

1. Paul wrote a **dax** on the board. "That **dax** is wrong," said Amanda. "Ten and ten make twenty. Not twelve!"

   A **dax** is:

   a letter — a word — a number

2. I **fize** at 12 Oak Street. Where do you **fize**?

   Fize is:

   go — live — like

3. My **mox** is brown and white. She likes milk.

   A **mox** is:

   a book — a mother — a cat

4. I can't find my **racot**. I put it on my desk. It's my blue one. I need it to do my drawing.

   A **racot** is:

   a coat — a pencil — a bicycle

5. Everyone liked that book about animals. The teacher **expolsed** it to the class.

   Expolsed is:

   read — spoke — made

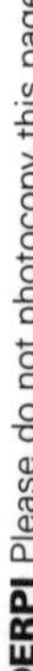

Unit 2

On This Day

Special Events

- Match each event with its picture on page 12 in your book.
- Write a letter from A to G on the line next to the event.

Graduation Day	________	Fête nationale	________
Father's Day	________	Helen Keller's birthday	________
World Environment Day	________	The first day of summer	________
Anne Frank's birthday	________		

- Write the name of the month on the calendar.
- Place the events on the calendar.

Sunday	Monday	Tuesday	Wednesday	Thursday	Friday	Saturday
		1	2	3	4	5 (G)
6	7	8	9	10	11	12 (C)
13 (A)	14	15	16	17	18	19
20	21 (F)	22	23	24 (D)	25 (E)	26
27 (B)	28	29	30			

- **I identified the special events.**
  All of them ☐ Most of them ☐ Some of them ☐ None of them ☐
- **I already knew about** ______________________________.
- **I learned about** ______________________________.

Extension Activity

June Celebrations

► Find out more about one of these special events.

Graduation Day

Father's Day

World Environment Day

Anne Frank's birthday

Fête nationale

Helen Keller's birthday

The first day of summer

I would like to find out more about ______________________________________.

I learned that ______________________________________

____

____

______________________________________.

Activity 1 Windows to the Past

SB 13

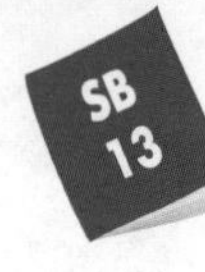

- Listen to the recording.
- Write the events on the timeline.

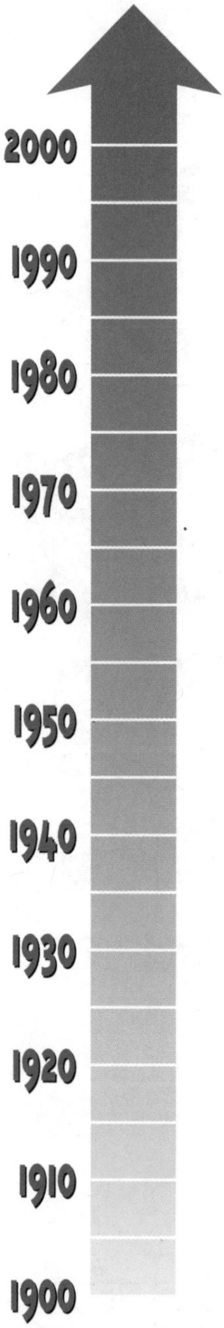
2000
1990
1980
1970
1960
1950
1940
1930
1920
1910
1900

- **I understood the news reports on the recording.**
  All of them ☐ Most of them ☐ Some of them ☐ None of them ☐
- **This activity was:**
  Very easy ☐ Easy ☐ Difficult ☐ Very difficult ☐

Flashback

- Read the texts on page 14 in your book.
- Write down the headline for each text.

Letter 1

____

____

Letter 2

____

____

E-mail message

____

____

Postcard

____

____

- **I found the key words in each text.**
  All of them ☐ Most of them ☐ Some of them ☐ None of them ☐
- **I learned something new in this activity.** Yes ☐ No ☐

Activity 3 A Cause for Celebration

SB 15

- Write how you celebrate your birthday.

____

____

- Make a candle for your birthday cake.
- Write your name and birthday on the candle.

Continued on next page

Activity 3 A Cause for Celebration (continued)

- Find out who shares your birthday month.
- Write their names on the birthday cake.

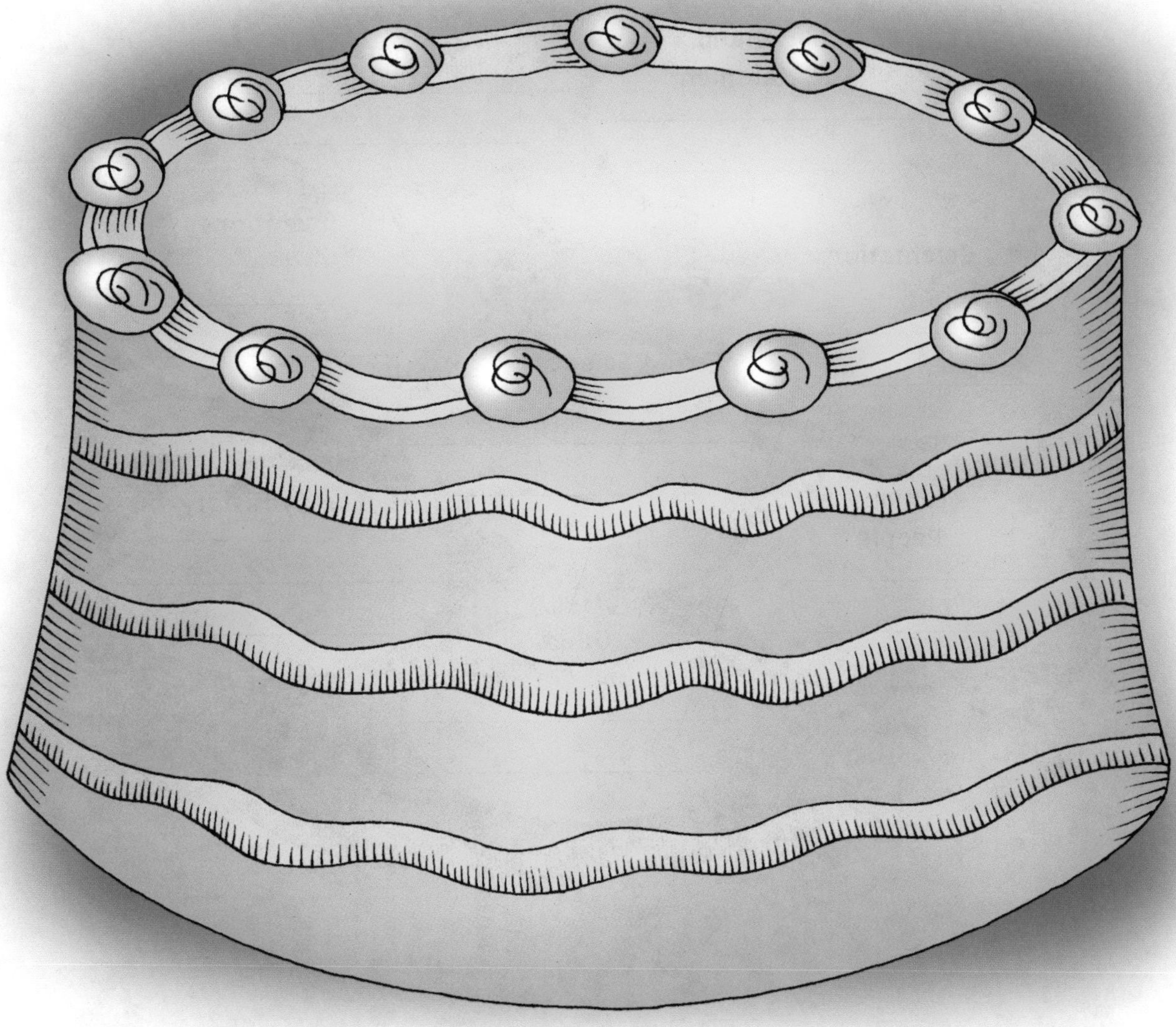

- I discovered which classmates share my birthday month. Yes ☐ No ☐
- I used Chatterbox 3 for help. Yes ☐ No ☐
- I spoke English during this activity.
  Always ☐ Most of the time ☐ Some of the time ☐ Never ☐

My Day in History

SB 16

- Find some events that happened on the date you were born.
- Place them in the appropriate category.

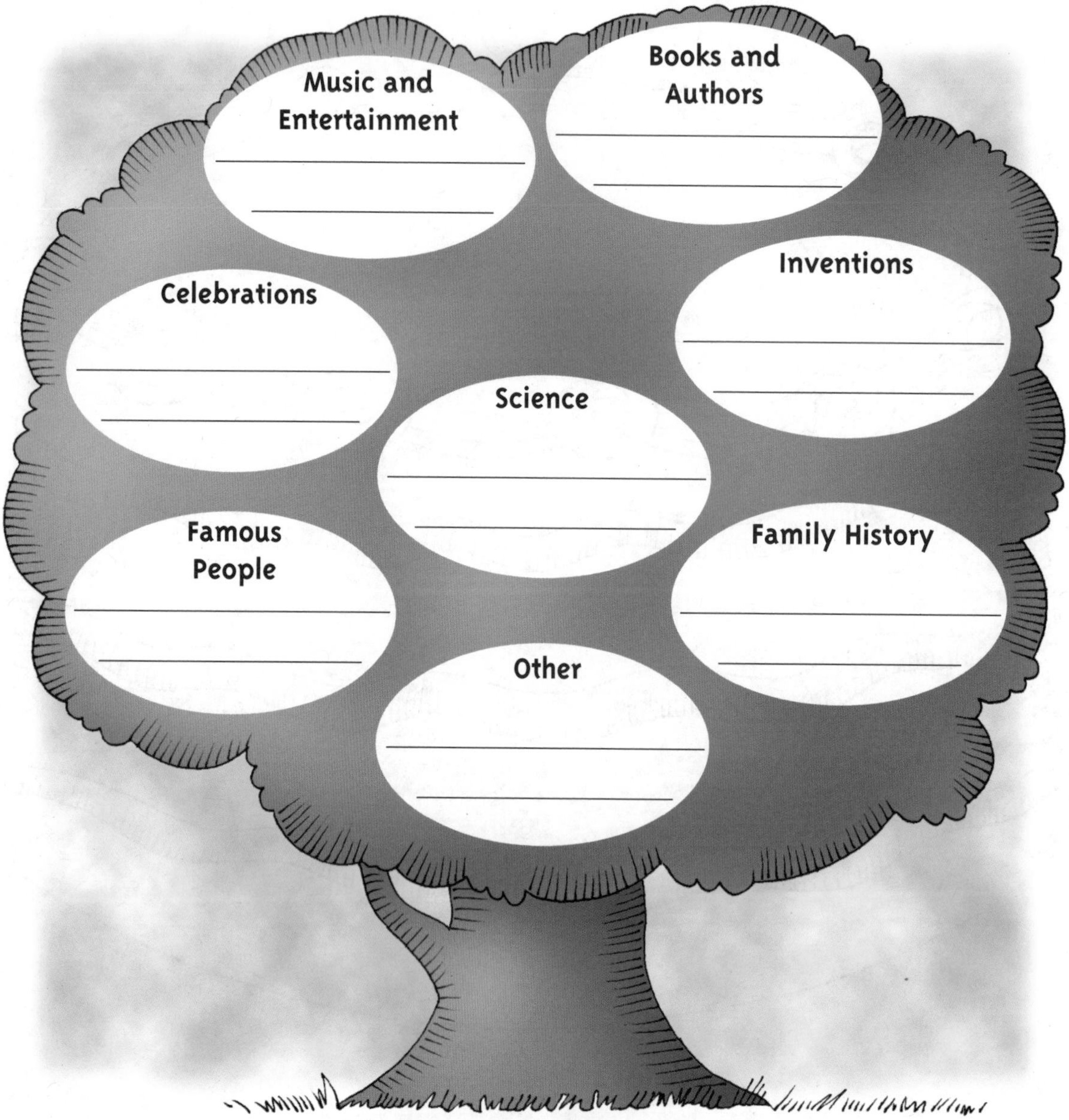

Music and Entertainment

____

____

Books and Authors

____

____

Celebrations

____

____

Inventions

____

____

Science

____

____

Famous People

____

____

Family History

____

____

Other

____

____

- I found three events that happened on my birthdate. Yes ☐ No ☐
- I used Chatterbox 2 for help. Yes ☐ No ☐
- This is where I found my information: ______________________.

Write down some events that happened on the date you were born.

- **I presented the events that happened on my birthdate.** Yes ☐ No ☐
- **I liked this unit.** Yes ☐ No ☐

Special Events

► Place each special event on the calendar.

January	February	March	April
______	______	______	______
______	______	______	______
May	**June**	**July**	**August**
______	______	______	______
______	______	______	______
September	**October**	**November**	**December**
______	______	______	______
______	______	______	______

Unit 3

Words of Honour

► **Match the pictures with the sentences.**

► **Write the numbers on the blank lines.**

(a) The lion is the most popular animal in heraldry.

____

(b) Heraldry started in the Middle Ages in Europe.

____

(c) Nobles could give a coat of arms to a peasant.

____

(d) Many different signs and symbols are used in heraldry.

____

(e) A coat of arms on a shield identified soldiers.

____

(f) Different colours and metals are used on a coat of arms.

____

- **I worked well with my partners.**
  Always ☐ Most of the time ☐ Some of the time ☐ Never ☐
- **I used Chatterbox 6 for help.** Yes ☐ No ☐

The Keeper

► **Colour Gladwin's coat of arms according to the description in the story.**

- **I understood the story.**
  All of it ☐ Most of it ☐ Some of it ☐ None of it ☐
- **I guessed the meaning of some words.** Yes ☐ No ☐
- **I liked ☐ didn't like ☐ the story because** ______________________________
  ______________________________.

Continued on next page

The Keeper (continued)

- Read the story.
- Answer the questions.

1. Who was with the man? ______ 2. What did he see in the distance? ______ 3. Why didn't he know if he could reach the village? ______ 4. Why did he pull the blanket over his head? ______	
1. Where did the man go when he reached the village? ______ 2. How did the people greet him at The Royal Lion? ______ 3. How did the man feel? ______	
1. What did the man do next? ______ 2. What did the innkeeper do? ______ 3. What did she give the man? ______ 4. What did the peasants discover about this man? ______	
1. What did the King give the innkeeper? Why? ______ ______ 2. What did the King decide to put on the coat of arms? ______ ______	

A New Beginning

- **Predict the beginning of the story "The Keeper."**
- **Answer the questions.**

Why was the king alone?

____

____

____

Where was he coming from?

____

____

____

What happened to the people he was with?

____

____

____

What's in a Name?

SB 25

► Read your text.

► Complete the chart with your partners.

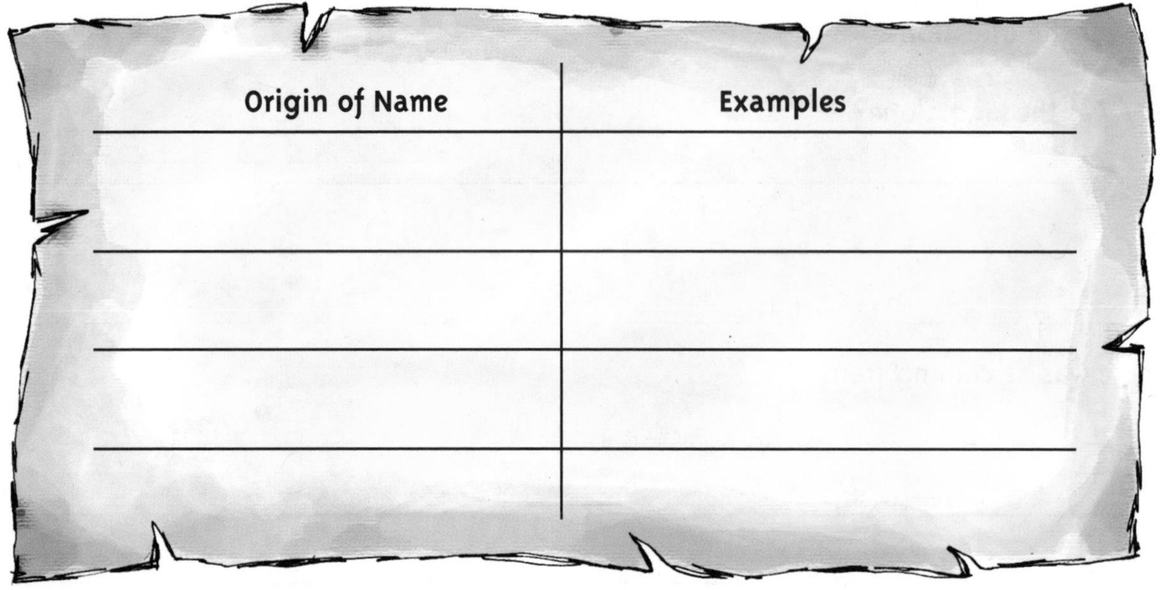

Origin of Name	Examples

► Read the list of names on page 25 in your book.

► Group the names by origin.

- I paid attention to my partners.
  Always ☐ Most of the time ☐ Some of the time ☐ Never ☐
- I shared information with my partners. Yes ☐ No ☐
- I used Chatterbox II for help. Yes ☐ No ☐

Extension Activity

The Origin of My Name

► **Find out the meaning and origin of your family name.**

My family name is

____

It comes from

____

____

____

It means

____

____

____

Heraldry: A Beginner's Guide

- Find the meaning of the objects and colours on Gladwin's coat of arms.
- Write why you think the King chose these objects and colours.

Object or Colour	Meaning	Reason

- **I discovered the meanings of the symbols.**
  All of them ☐ Most of them ☐ Some of them ☐ None of them ☐

Activity 4 Words to Live By

► Invent your personal motto.

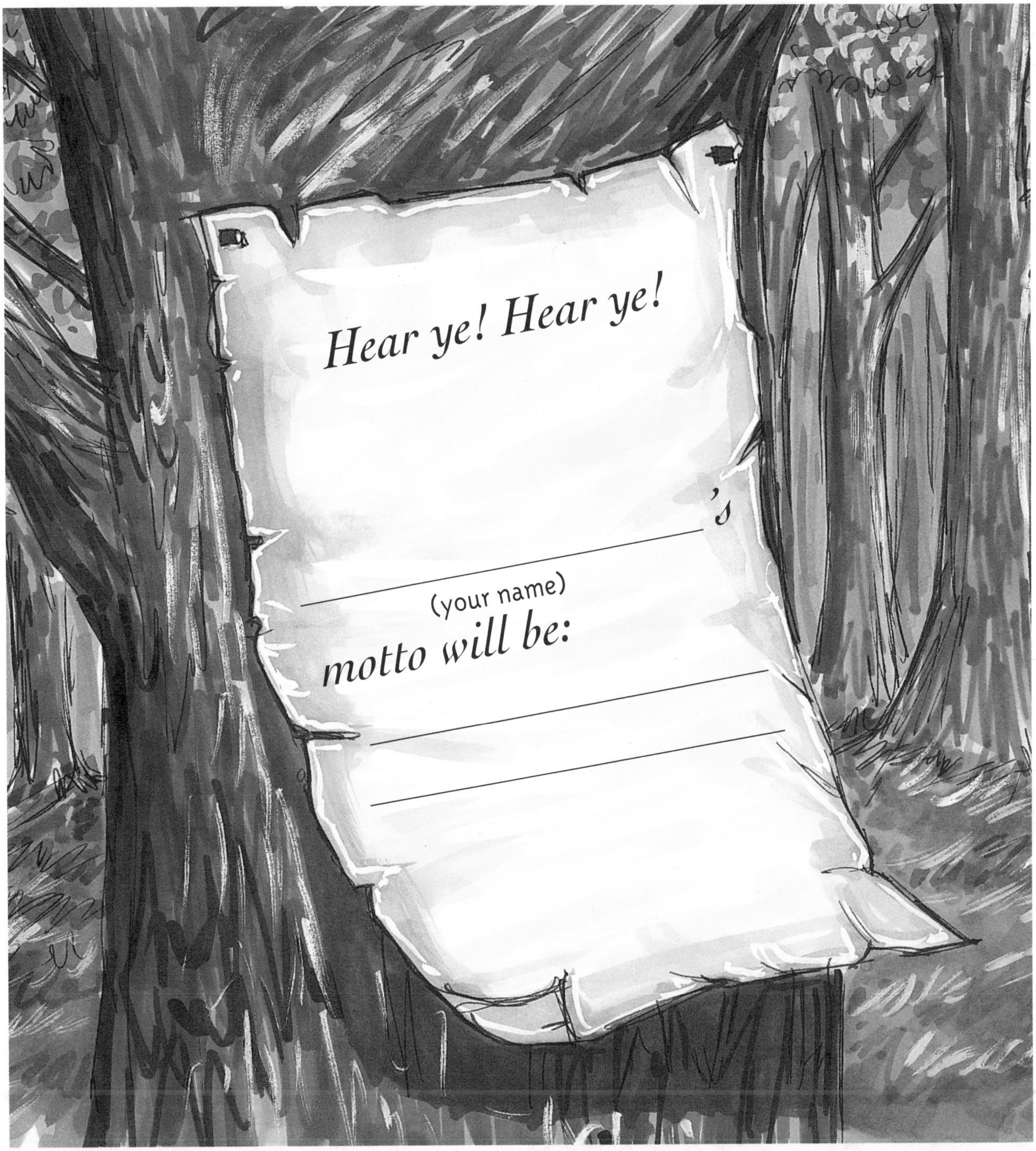

Hear ye! Hear ye!

_______________________'s
(your name)

motto will be:

____

____

- **I understood the mottoes.**
  All of them ☐ Most of them ☐ Some of them ☐ None of them ☐
- **I wrote my own motto with ☐ or without ☐ help.**

► Plan your personal coat of arms.

► Choose the shape of your coat of arms.

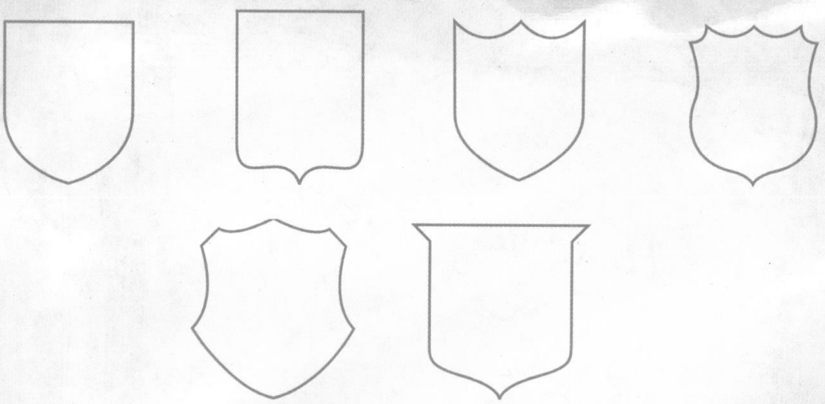

► Identify four of your qualities.

► Find the symbols that represent these qualities.

► Choose the colours or metals for the background and symbols.

- **I am satisfied with my coat of arms.**
  Extremely ☐ Very ☐ Not very ☐ Not at all ☐
- **During this unit, I worked:**
  Very hard ☐ Moderately hard ☐ Not very hard ☐ Not hard at all ☐

Extension Activity

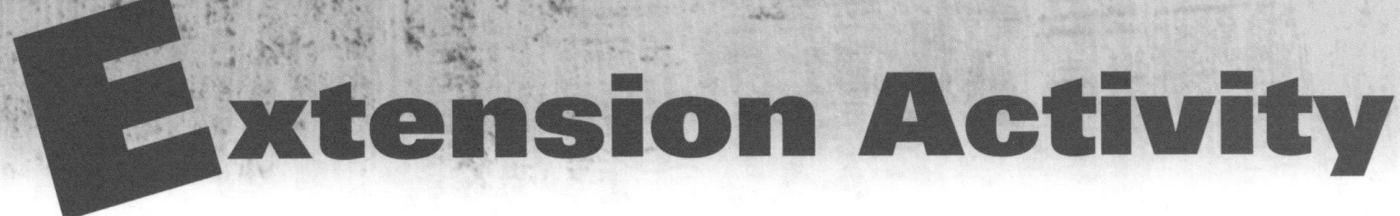

My Own Coat of Arms

- Find out if your family has a coat of arms.
- Draw a picture of it.

Extra Activity

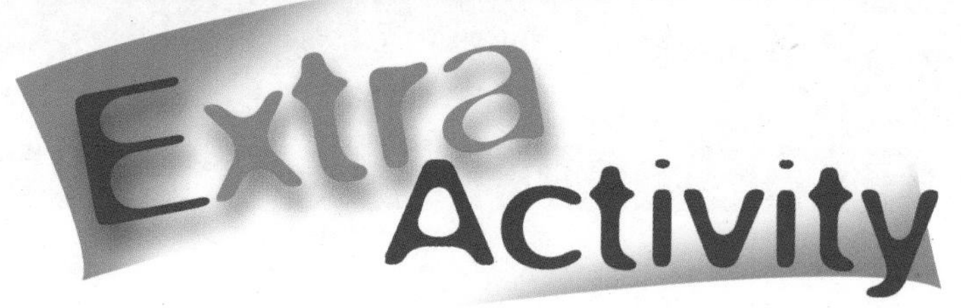

Celebrating Celebrities

- Think of a famous person you admire.
- Design a coat of arms for this person.

- Write down why you chose the symbols and colours for this person.

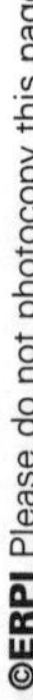

Unit 4

Playing Around

Warm-up

SB 32

- Name as many toys as you can.
- Label the toys.

- I helped my partners find the names of the toys and games. Yes ☐ No ☐
- I was able to identify the toys and games.
  All of them ☐ Most of them ☐ Some of them ☐ None of them ☐

Timeless Toys

- Write the name of each item described in Otto's letter.
- Find the picture and write its letter in the appropriate place.
- Find a modern version for each item.

	Item	Then	Now
1.			
2.			
3.			
4.			
5.			

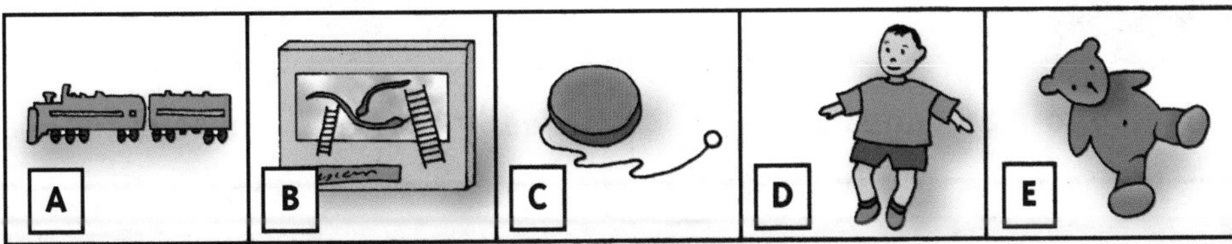

- **I named the items described in the letter.**
  All of them ☐ Most of them ☐ Some of them ☐ None of them ☐
- **I found the key words in the descriptions.** Yes ☐ No ☐
- **I found a modern version for each toy.** Yes ☐ No ☐

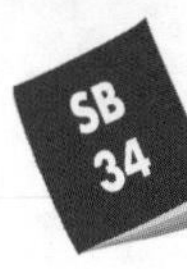

Activity 2 A Place for Everything

SB 34

- Write the names of the toys that go in each toy box.
- Suggest some more toys for each toy box.

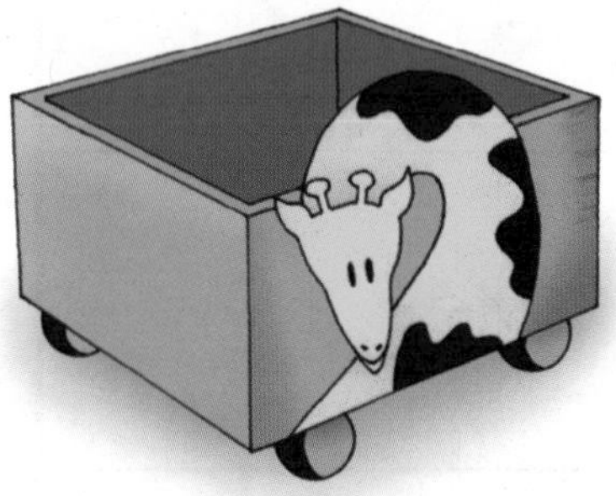

Toys for tots (ages 0 to 2)

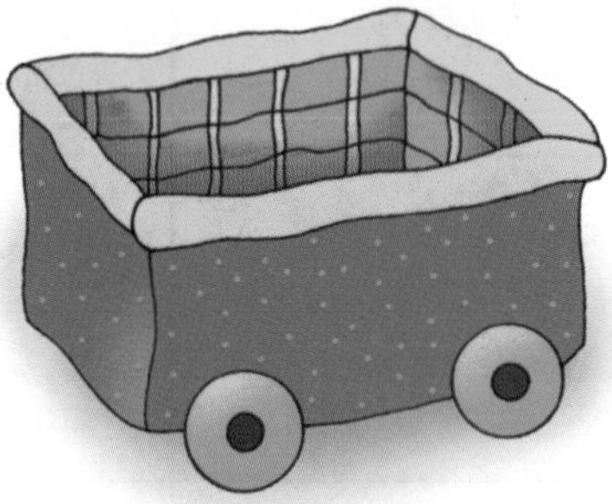

I'm a big kid now! (ages 2 to 5)

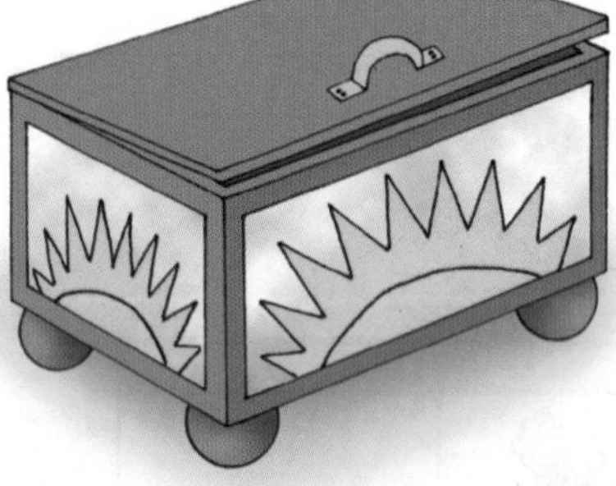

Older kids like to play (ages 6 to 12)

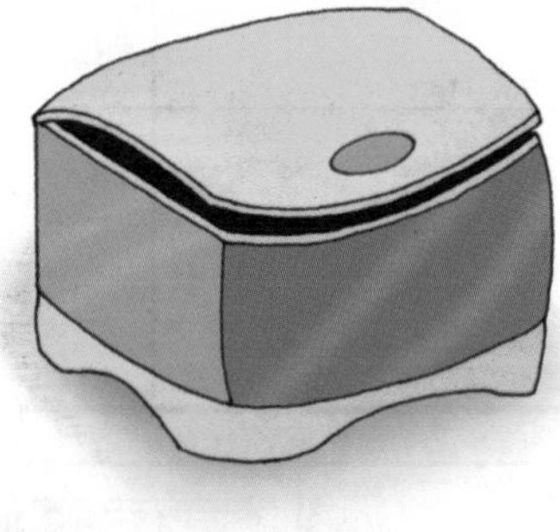

Really big kids like toys too! (age 12+)

- **I worked well with my partners.**
  Always ☐ Most of the time ☐ Some of the time ☐ Never ☐
- **I spoke English during this activity.**
  Always ☐ Most of the time ☐ Some of the time ☐ Never ☐
- **I shared my opinion with my partners.** Yes ☐ No ☐

Toys! Toys! Toys!

SB 35

► Listen to the ads.

► Put the pictures in order.

- **I understood the advertisements.**
  All of them ☐ Most of them ☐ Some of them ☐ None of them ☐
- **I was able to put the pictures in order.** Yes ☐ No ☐

Something Old, Something New

SB 36

► **With your partner, select a toy to remodel.**

We will remodel:

___

► **Make a sketch of your toy.**

- **I spoke English during this activity.**
  Always ☐ Most of the time ☐ Some of the time ☐ Never ☐
- **I used Chatterbox 9 for help.** Yes ☐ No ☐

Draw a picture of your new toy.

Write the advertisement to present your new toy.

Remember to use:

- an adjective to describe your product ☐
- an adjective ending in -able ☐
- an advertising expression ☐

- I listened carefully to my classmates' presentations. Yes ☐ No ☐
- I worked well with my partner.
  Always ☐ Most of the time ☐ Some of the time ☐ Never ☐

What Am I?

- Read the clues.
- Guess which popular toy is being described.

1. These first appeared in North America in 1903.
   A child uses 730 of these before the age of ten.
   They come in 120 colours.

   ____

2. Children played with these in Babylon in 2000 BC.
   They are usually decorated.
   They whistle when they turn.

   ____

3. These were invented in China.
   There are four symbols on them.
   Each one represents one week of the year.

   ____

4. These were invented in 3000 BC.
   They were made of clay, stone, wood or glass.
   One of them is called a "shooter."

   ____

Unit 5

Fear Files

Warm-up

SB 40

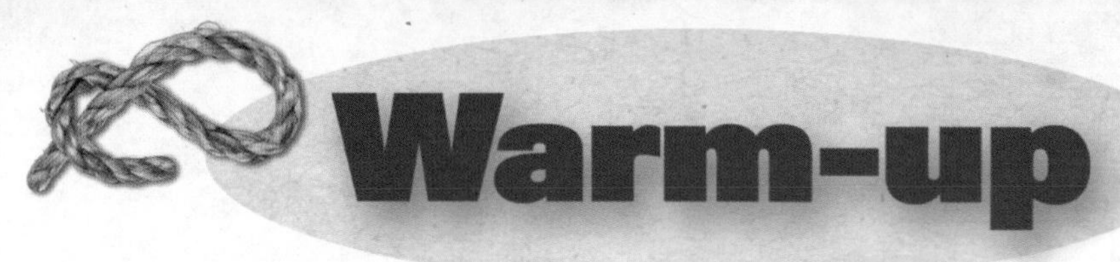

Name some fears.

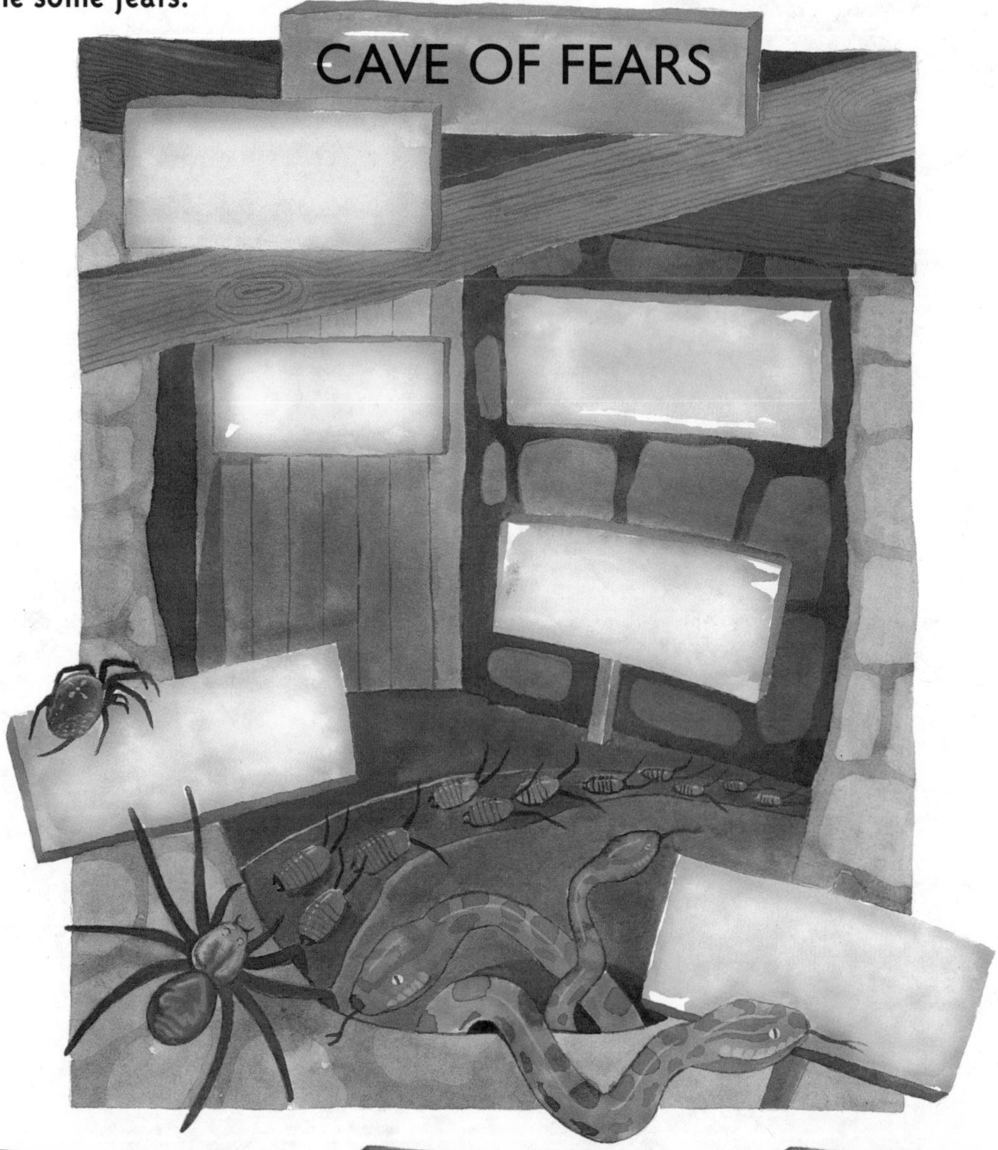

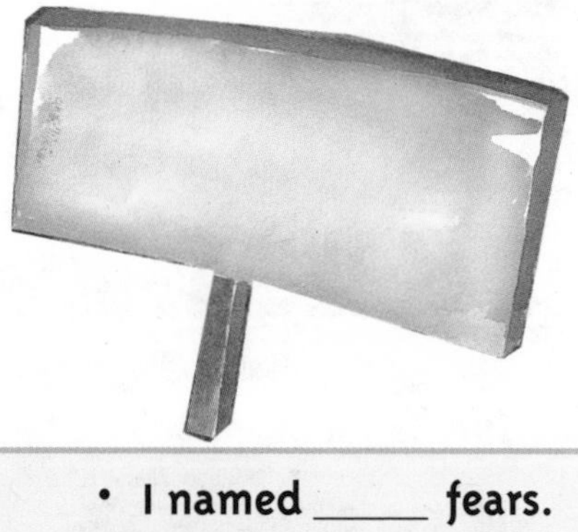

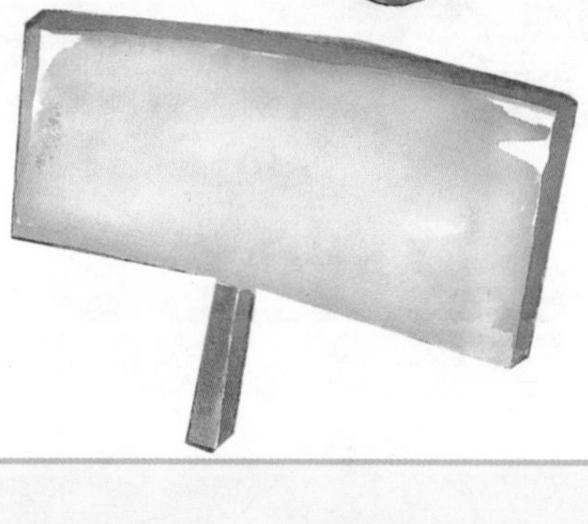

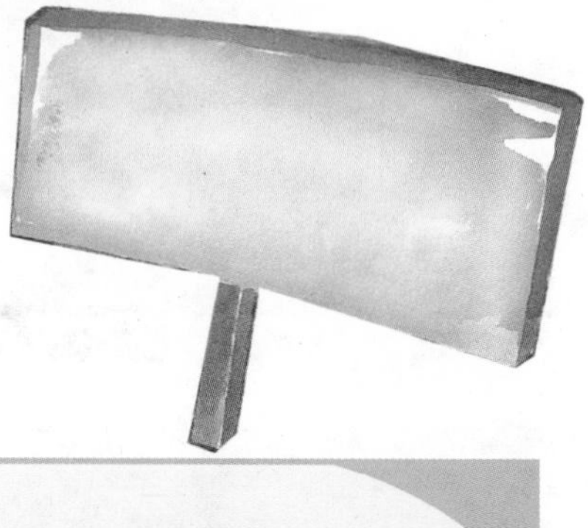

- I named _____ fears.
- This activity was:
  Very easy ☐ Easy ☐ Difficult ☐ Very difficult ☐

Activity 1

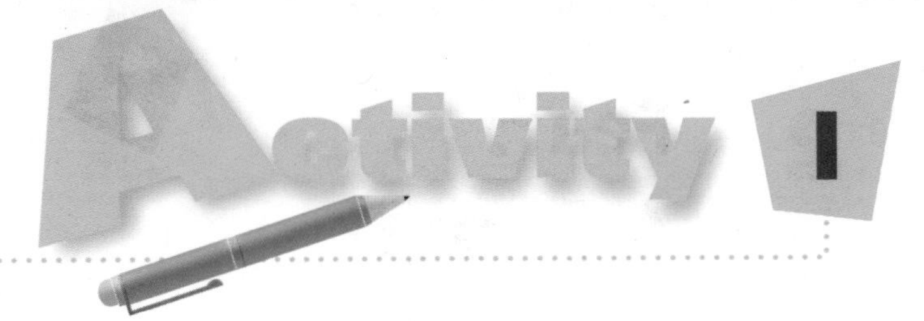

The Physical Signs of Fear

SB 41

- Write what happens when you feel afraid.
- Fill in the blanks.

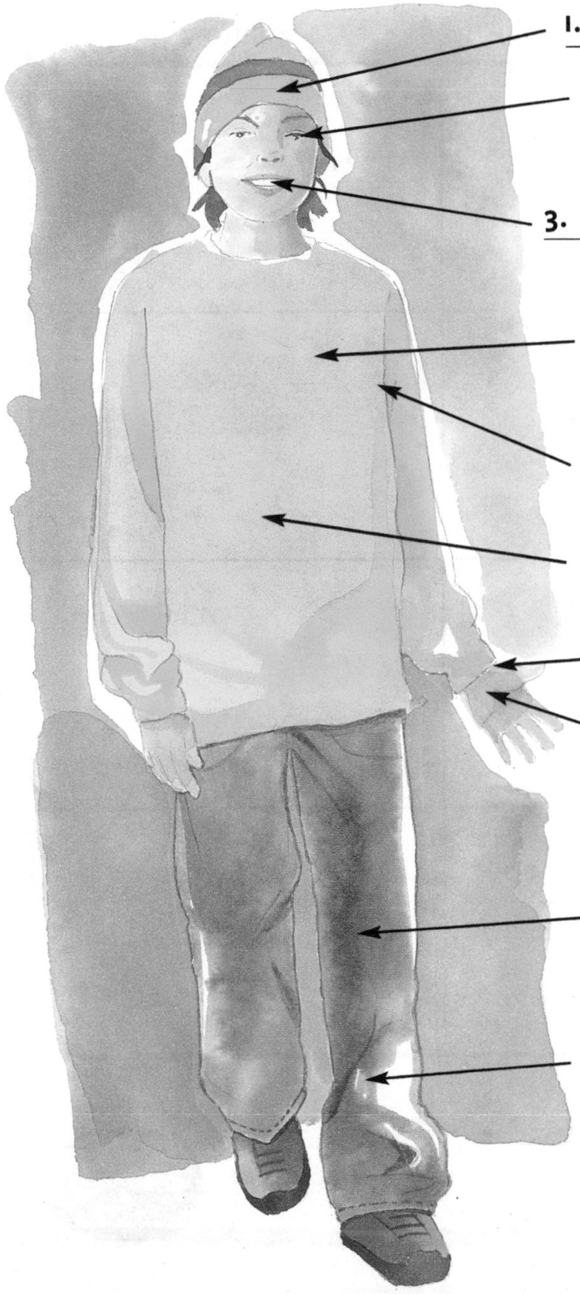

1. ______________________________
2. ______________________________
3. ______________________________
4. ______________________________
5. ______________________________
6. ______________________________
7. ______________________________
8. ______________________________
9. ______________________________
10. ______________________________

- **I understood the text.** Yes ☐ No ☐
- **I wrote down the physical signs of fear.**
  All of them ☐ Most of them ☐ Some of them ☐ None of them ☐

Activity 2 Fear: A Report

- Listen to the interviews.
- Complete the chart.

Name	Age	Fear	Symptom	Solution
Floyd				
Vivian				
Helga				
Greg				

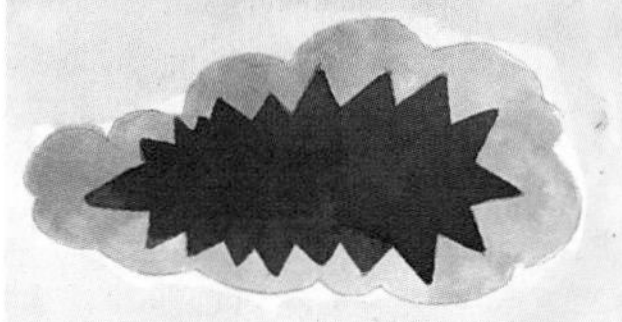

- I understood the interviews. Yes ☐ No ☐
- I completed the chart with ☐ or without ☐ help.

A Story of Fear

- Write your own version of the story.
- For each number, choose one of the options listed on the index card below.

The night was ____________[1]. I walked slowly down the ____________[2] road. My heart was beating very fast. I was so ____________[3]. Suddenly I heard a sound. What was it? A ____________[4]? My foot hit something. It moved. ____________![5] Oh, no! A ____________[6]? I jumped. I tried to ____________[7] but I couldn't. My ____________[8] were shaking. Then I saw the thing clearly. It was ____________[9]. Finally I ran away. I am so afraid of ____________[10]!

1. dark, stormy, rainy
2. lonely, long, dark
3. afraid, scared, terrified
4. bat, bear, wolf
5. Look out! Watch out! Be careful!
6. snake, rat, tarantula
7. scream, run, escape
8. knees, hands, legs
9. ugly, enormous, angry
10. skunks, squirrels, cats

- I used Chatterbox 15 for help. Yes ☐ No ☐
- I wrote my own story. Yes ☐ No ☐
- I am happy with the story I wrote.
  Extremely ☐ Very ☐ Not very ☐ Not at all ☐

Another Story of Fear

► **Read the story.**

The room was small and very dirty. Rats ran across the floor. The door was locked. I was alone. My hands started to shake. I saw a note on the table. It said, "Be careful! You are in danger!"

Suddenly I heard a noise behind me. I turned around and saw an enormous wolf. I began to scream. I was so afraid. Then I heard a voice shouting, "Wake up! It's time to go to school." Phew!

► **Now fill in the blanks to create a new story.**

The room was ______________ and very ______________. ______________ ran across the floor. The door was locked. I was ______________. ______________ started to shake. I saw a note on the table. It said, " ______________ ! You are in danger!"

Suddenly I heard a ______________ behind me. I turned around and saw ________________________. I began ______________. I was so ______________. Then I heard a voice shouting, "Wake up! It's time to go to school." Phew!

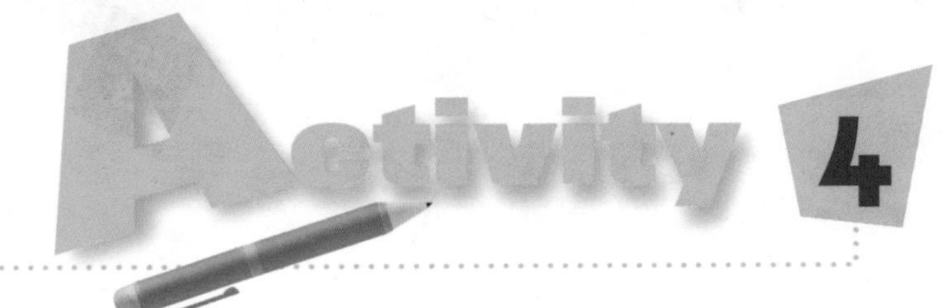

Activity 4 Finding Fears

SB 44

- Interview four people about their fears.
- Record your results on the chart.

Name	Age	Fear	Symptom	Solution

- I interviewed _____ people.
- This activity was fun. Yes ☐ No ☐

Wrap-up

SB 45

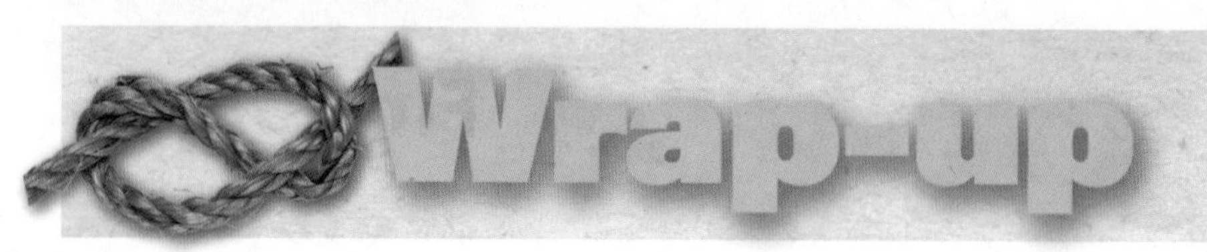

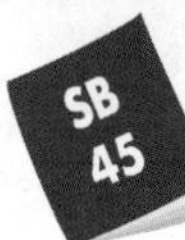

Plan your Cave of Fears on this page.

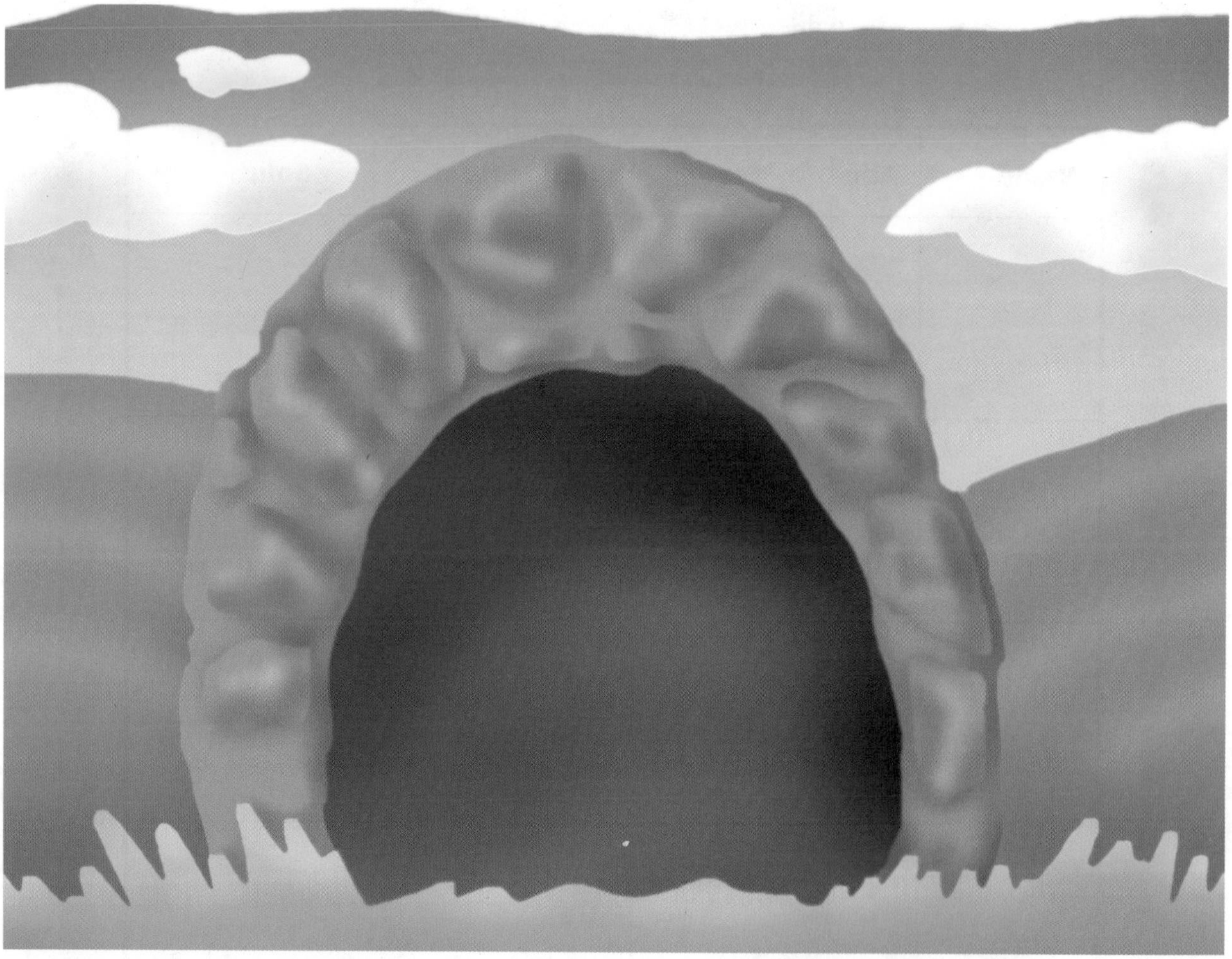

- **I spoke English during this activity.**
  Always ☐ Most of the time ☐ Some of the time ☐ Never ☐
- **I am satisfied with my work.**
  Extremely ☐ Very ☐ Not very ☐ Not at all ☐

A Circle of Fear

- Think of two other things you fear the most.
- Draw them in the circle below.
- Add them to your Cave of Fears.

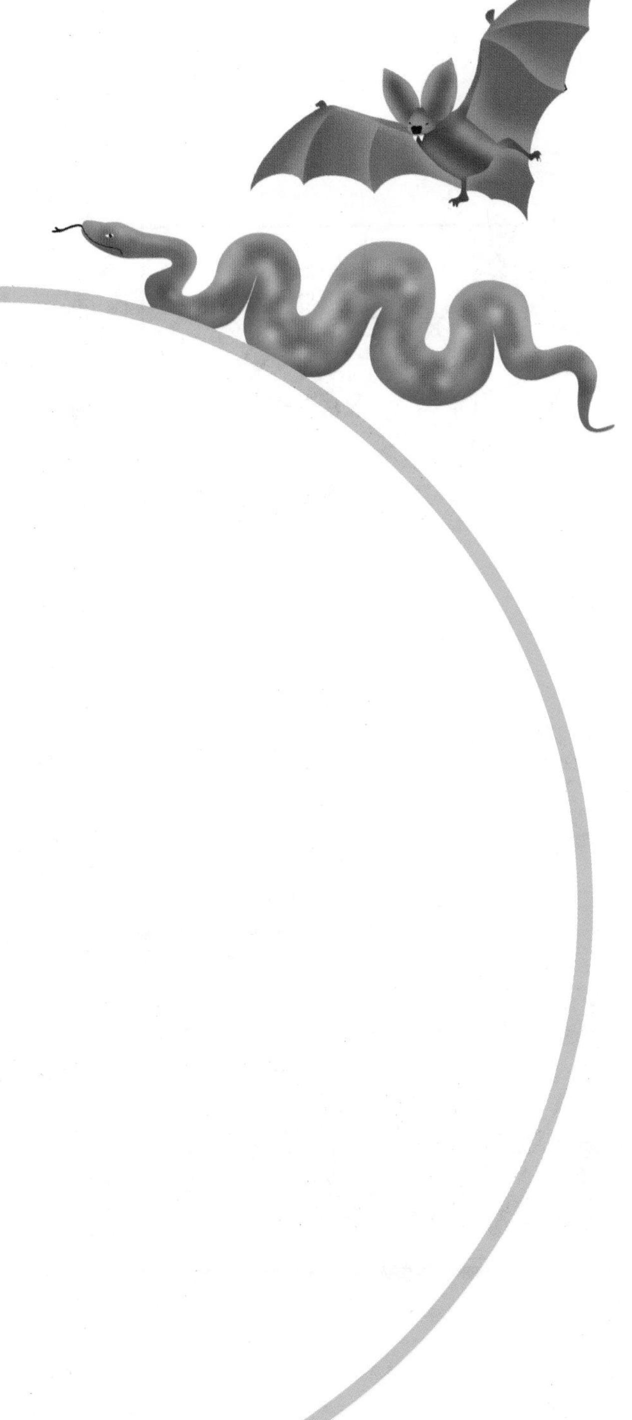

My Scariest Things

- Look at the four categories.
- Write what scares you the most in each category.

Unit 6

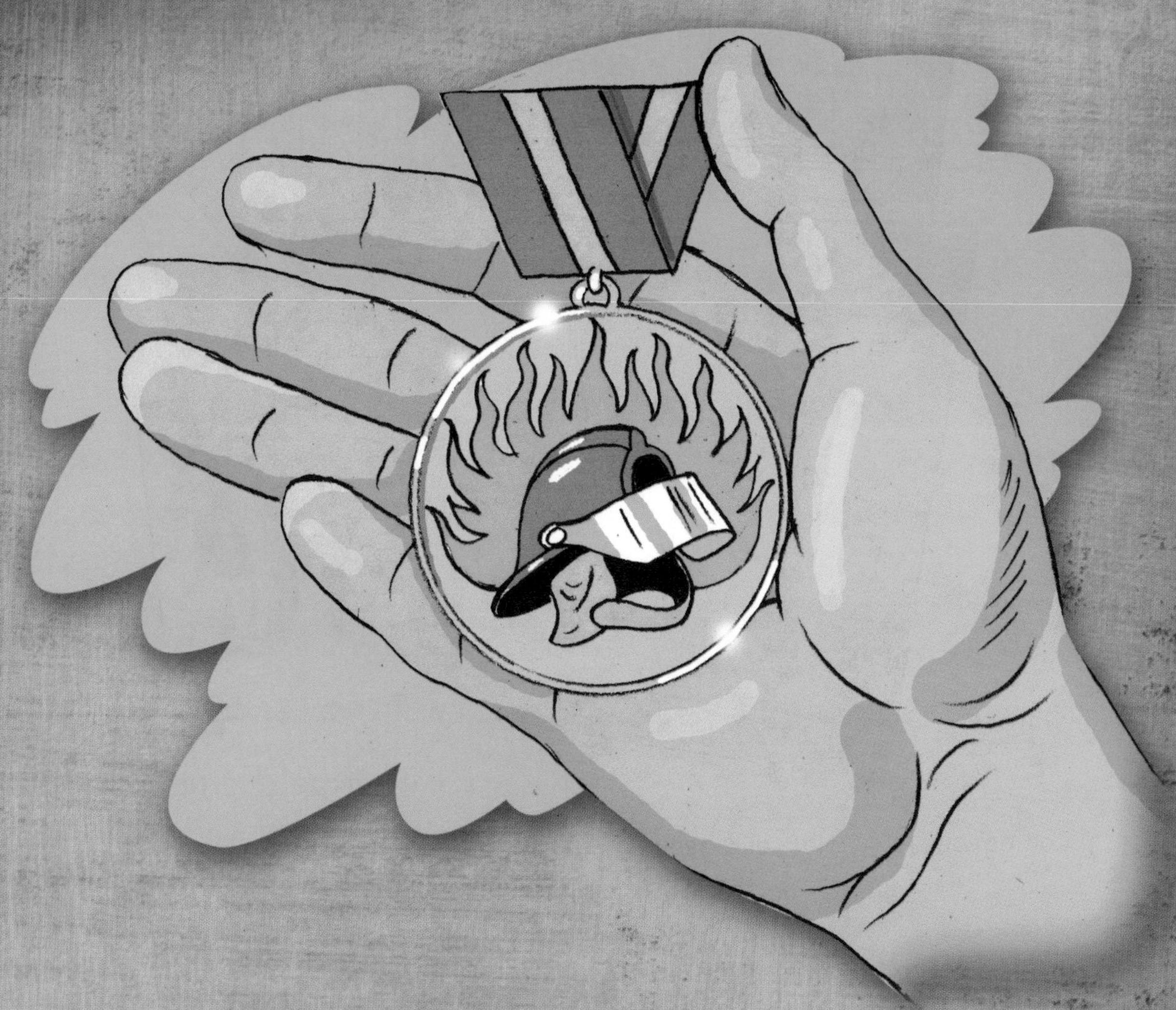

It Takes Courage

► **Identify the pictures that show acts of courage.**

2. Courageous ☐ Not courageous ☐

1. Courageous ☐ Not courageous ☐

4. Courageous ☐ Not courageous ☐

3. Courageous ☐ Not courageous ☐

► **Describe some other acts of courage.**

____

____

- **I understand what courage means.** Yes ☐ No ☐
- **I can name some courageous actions.** Yes ☐ No ☐

Down Under

Answer the questions before listening to the story.

1. What is the title of the story? ______________________
2. Who are the main characters? ______________________
3. Where does the story take place? ______________________
4. What do you think the theme of the story is?

love ☐ recklessness ☐ courage ☐ honesty ☐

Listen to the first part of the story.

Check off your answers.

1.	Orpheus and Eurydice got married.	True ☐	False ☐
2.	Eurydice was bitten by a snake.	True ☐	False ☐
3.	Eurydice immediately fell asleep.	True ☐	False ☐
4.	Orpheus decided to bring Eurydice back from the World of the Dead.	True ☐	False ☐

Predict the ending of the story.

I think Orpheus:

— will be able to bring Eurydice back from the World of the Dead. ☐

— won't be able to bring Eurydice back from the World of the Dead. ☐

— won't be able to return from the World of the Dead. ☐

— will meet another woman, fall in love and get married again. ☐

Continued on next page

Down Under (continued)

► **Listen to the last part of the story.**

► **Write the names of the characters and state who they are.**

	____________________	____________________
	____________________	____________________
	____________________	____________________
	____________________	____________________
	____________________	____________________

► **Place the events in order.**

_____ A. Orpheus decided to bring Eurydice back from the World of the Dead.

_____ B. Orpheus and Eurydice walked back through a dark tunnel.

_____ C. Orpheus heard a cry and turned to Eurydice, who disappeared forever.

_____ D. Orpheus charmed Cerberus and entered the World of the Dead.

_____ E. Orpheus and Eurydice loved each other and decided to get married.

_____ F. Orpheus convinced Hades to let Eurydice return to the Land of the Living.

_____ G. Orpheus promised not to look at Eurydice until they were out of the World of the Dead.

_____ H. Orpheus crossed the River Styx after charming Charon.

_____ I. On their wedding day, Eurydice stepped on a poisonous snake and died instantly.

- **I was able to identify the characters, setting and theme of the story.** Yes ☐ No ☐
- **I understood the main events of the story.**
  All of them ☐ Most of them ☐ Some of them ☐ None of them ☐

Activity 2 A Model of Courage

► Answer the questions.

Who is this person?

____

Why did she begin to swim every day?

____

What sport did she discover?

____

What has she won?

____

Which competitions has she participated in?

____

► Write why you think she is a hero.

____

____

____

- I understood the text about Chantal Petitclerc.

All of it ☐ Most of it ☐ Some of it ☐ None of it ☐

Face Your Fears

► **Match each letter with its solution.**

Newville Elementary Monthly News

Tell your fears to Dr Fear

Dear Dr Fear,

After school my friends are teaching me tricks to do on my bicycle. Yesterday I fell. Now I am afraid to get hurt again. What should I do?

Dear Dr Fear,

All the girls in my class are getting tattoos. I think they look silly. It's not what I want to do. But I want to be like the other kids. Can I still be cool without a tattoo?

Dear Dr Fear,

I have to wear glasses. I am too shy to wear them. I always carry them in my schoolbag.

The problem is: I can't see without them. Next week I have a big test. Will my friends laugh at me if I wear my glasses?

6

Dear Friend,

Courage comes in many forms. It takes courage to believe in your friends. They will not laugh at you if they are true friends. They will understand. Write your test. Wear your glasses. Your eyes are very important.

Dear Friend,

You are right to worry about getting hurt again. Wear a helmet, elbow pads and knee pads. Don't be reckless. Be safe! Your friends may follow your example.

Dear Friend,

Stand up for what you want. Don't be afraid to be different. Be you!

• **I found a solution to each problem.** Yes ☐ No ☐

Extension Activity

Nicholas's Problem

► **Read the letter to Dr Fear.**

Dear Dr Fear,

I have a big problem. I like a girl in my class and I want her to like me. Her name is Yulan. She's an excellent swimmer. Last week she won a bronze medal.

Next week our class is going to the pool. I don't know how to swim and I'm afraid of the water. Yulan will surely laugh at me. This will ruin my chances with her. What should I do?

Sincerely,

Nicholas

► **Answer the questions.**

1. What is the girl's name? ______________________
2. What is she good at? ______________________
3. What is Nicholas's problem? ______________________
____
4. What should Nicholas do?
   a) Pretend he can swim and dive into the deep end.
   b) Pretend he has a cold and sit on a bench near the pool.
   c) Tell Yulan he is afraid of the water.
   d) Ask Yulan to teach him how to swim.

► **Write a letter in response to Nicholas.**

____

____

____

____

____

A Medal of Courage

► **Read the nominations.**

Sheila MacDonald My grandmother's husband died when she was thirty-four years old. She had nine young children to support. She decided to manage my grandfather's store. Everyone was against the idea. This decision took a lot of courage. She raised her family and worked full-time. She overcame all the obstacles and became a successful business woman.	
Pamela Green-Ladouceur My younger sister has a learning disability. She has trouble speaking and writing. Her dream was to become a baker. She was sure she could succeed. She studied hard and never gave up. She finally received her diploma. She now works in an excellent restaurant and makes the best cheesecake in town.	
Vijay Musharraf and King My cousin trained his dog King very well. Last summer, King saved me from drowning. I was swimming in a river with a strong current. Suddenly I couldn't get back to shore. My cousin told King to go and get me. King immediately jumped into the water. I held on to his neck as he swam back to shore. King and my cousin are terrific!	

Continued on next page

A Medal of Courage (continued)

William Hunter

My father is a firefighter. He has to take many risks. He often has to enter buildings that are on fire. Every time there is a fire, my dad hopes that there won't be any victims. Sometimes it's too late and some people die. This makes my dad very sad. I'm very proud of my father because he has saved many lives.

► **Decide who should receive the medal.**

The winner of the medal is ______________________ because ______________

____.

- **My presentation of the nominee was:**
  Excellent ☐ Very good ☐ Not very good ☐ Not good at all ☐
- **I used Chatterbox 6 for help in the group discussion.** Yes ☐ No ☐

► Write some facts about a person you admire.

► Choose someone you admire. Find some facts about this person.

What?

____
____
____
____

When?

____
____
____
____

Who?

____
____
____
____

Where?

____
____
____
____

Why?

____
____
____
____

Continued on next page

Wrap-up (continued)

► **Write the draft of your text about your hero.**

- **The text I wrote about my hero was:**
  Excellent ☐ Very good ☐ Not very good ☐ Not good at all ☐
- **I am satisfied with the presentation I gave about my hero.**
  Extremely ☐ Very ☐ Not very ☐ Not at all ☐

They Made a Difference

- Read the descriptions.
- Match each description with its picture.

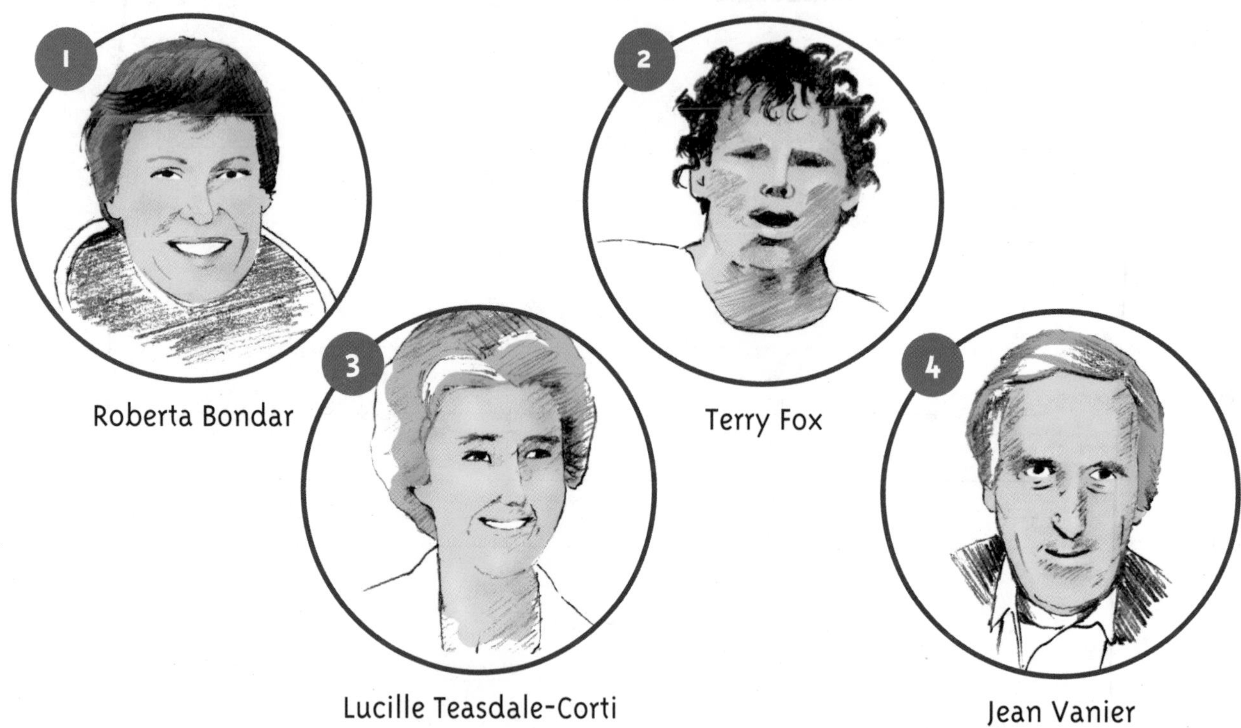

At the age of 18, he discovered that he had cancer in his right leg. In 1980, he ran across Canada on a journey he called the Marathon of Hope. He raised over $24 million for cancer research. ______

After a brilliant career in the army, he founded a centre to take care of adults with developmental disabilities. Built in 1964, the centre was called L'Arche. There are now over one hundred of these centres around the world. ______

She joined the Canadian Space Program in 1983. In 1992, she flew on the space shuttle Discovery to perform experiments. She was the first Canadian woman in space. ______

She graduated from Université de Montréal in 1955. She became one of the first woman surgeons in Québec. She and her husband built a modern hospital and a school of nursing in Uganda. ______

Unit 7

Beat the Record

Name Those Records!

► **Write the record beside the picture.**

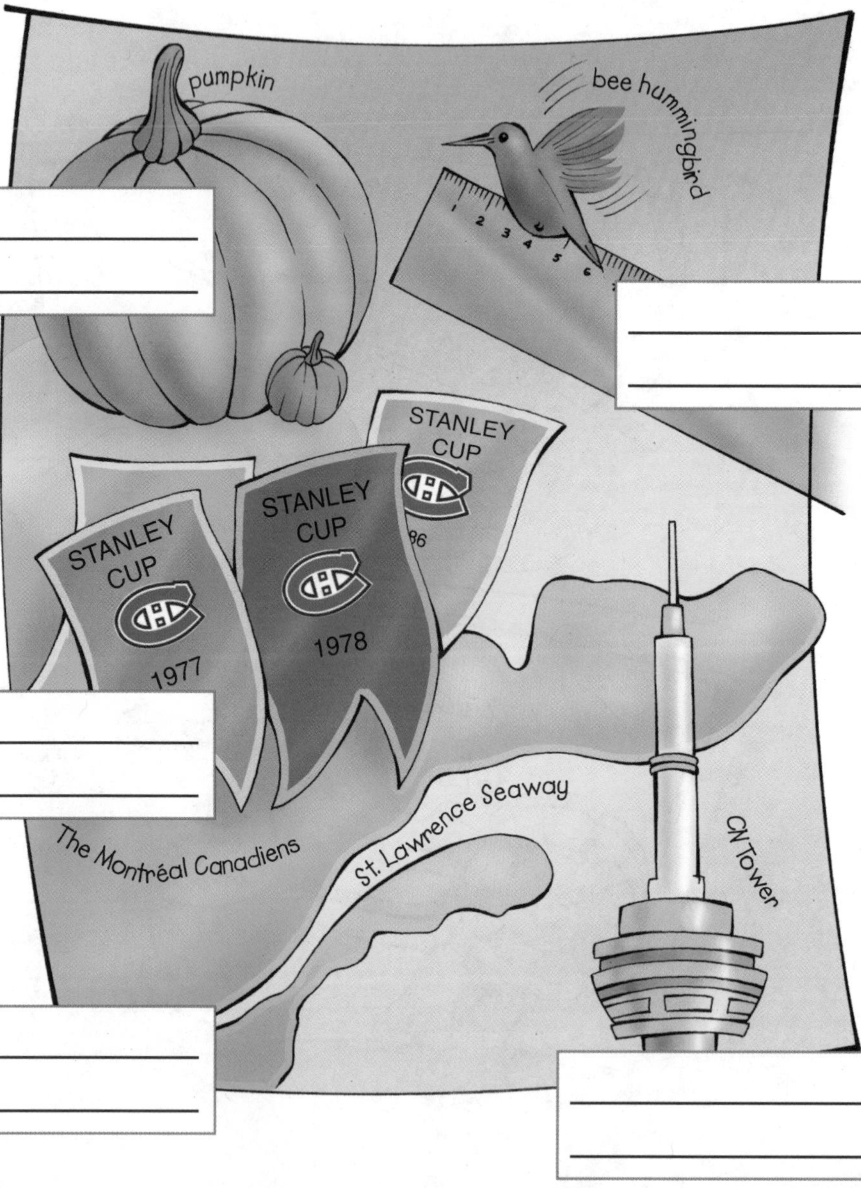

pumpkin

bee hummingbird

STANLEY CUP

STANLEY CUP 1977

STANLEY CUP 1978

The Montréal Canadiens

St. Lawrence Seaway

CN Tower

• **I identified ________ world records.**

Activity 1 Kids on Record

► **Complete the following records.**

Event	Record holder
Fastest crossword team	
Loudest whistle	
Biggest bubble	
Longest list	

► **Survey your classmates and add their suggestions to this list.**

► **Find the record holder in your group.**

Event	Record holder
Shortest pencil	
Most knots in a shoelace	
Most CDs at home	

- **I made a list of ________ records with my partner.**
- **I spoke English during this activity.**
  Always ☐ Most of the time ☐ Some of the time ☐ Never ☐

Who Did What?

► **Write about the record holders.**

► **Complete the sentences.**

______________ ______________

the biggest bubble.

______________ ______________

the longest list.

______________ ______________

the loudest whistle.

____

______________ their puzzle first.

For the Record

- **Find some more record holders.**
- **Ask your classmates these questions.**
- **Identify the record holder in each category.**

  - How many pets do you have?
  - How many telephones are there in your house?
  - How many brothers do you have?
  - How many sisters do you have?
  - How many aunts and uncles do you have?

most pets
most telephones
most brothers
most sisters
most aunts and uncles

Name	Pets	Telephones	Brothers	Sisters	Aunts and uncles

Set Your Own Record!

► Record your partners' results.

Name	Time	Rank

► Make a bar graph to show the results.

- I helped my partners make a bar graph. Yes ☐ No ☐
- I spoke English during this activity. Yes ☐ No ☐

Plan Your Event

► Complete the planning form.

Planning Form

Group members: ____________________ ____________________

____________________ ____________________

Event: ____

____

Materials required: ____

____

____

____

Rules: ____

____

____

____

- I helped make the rules for an event. Yes ☐ No ☐
- I used Chatterbox 5 for help. Yes ☐ No ☐

Activity 4 Ready, Steady, Go!

SB 62

► **Plan what you will write on the certificate.**

Beat-the-Record Certificate

To: ______________________________

For: ______________________________

From: ______________________________

Congratulations!

- I used Chatterbox 1 for help. Yes ☐ No ☐
- I participated in ________ events.
- My favourite event was: ______________________________.

► Complete the following checklist.

► Copy it and add it to your section of the Class Record Book.

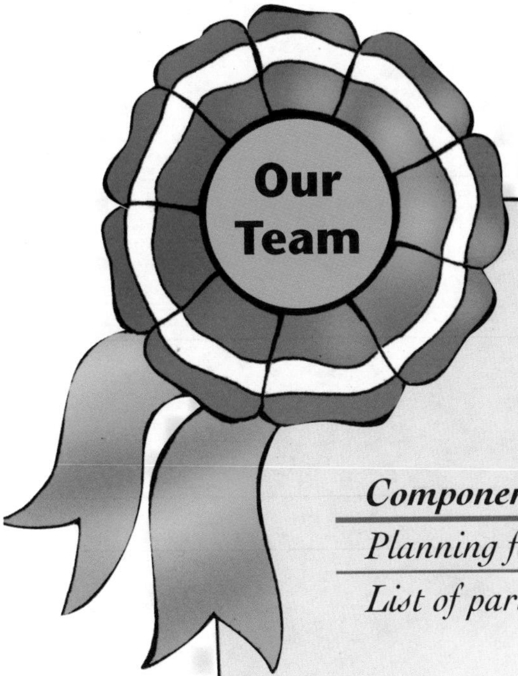

Our Team

Component	✓
Planning form	
List of participants: ____________________ ____________________ ____________________ ____________________	
Bar graph	
Name of record holder: ____________________	

- **During this unit, I worked:**
  Very hard ☐ Hard ☐ Not very hard ☐ Not hard at all ☐

World Records

- Look for world records on the Internet or in library books.
- Start with these and add others.

1. The tallest totem pole (Canada):

2. The most Oscars:

3. The biggest spider:

4. The highest waterfall:

5. The largest shopping centre:

6. The youngest author:

7.

8.

Unit 8

Celebrating the World

Around the World

- Trace Paul and Paulette's journey on the map.
- Draw a line from country to country.

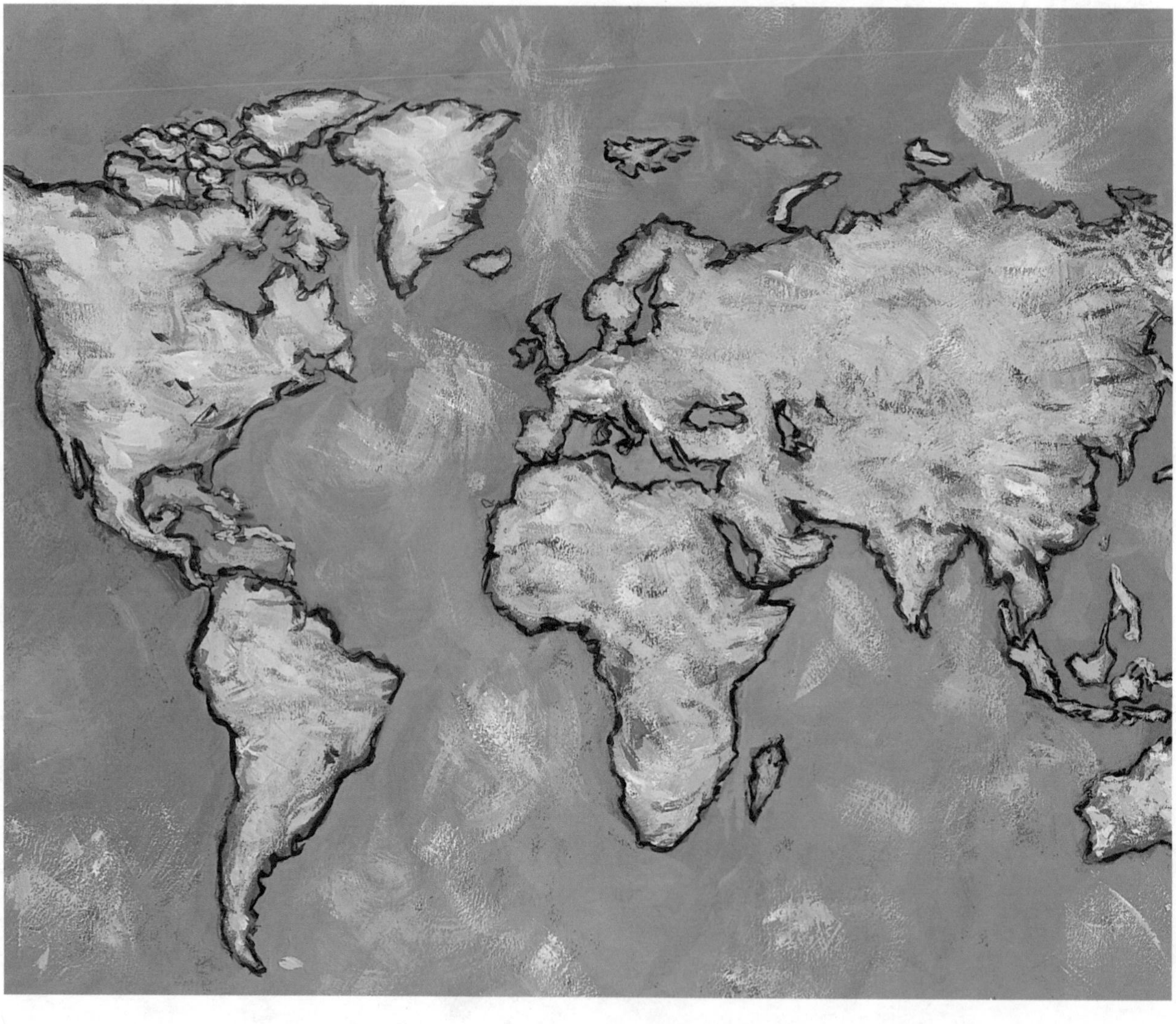

- I identified ________ places on the brochures.
- I named the celebrations. Yes ☐ No ☐
- I was able to trace Paul and Paulette's journey on the map. Yes ☐ No ☐

May Day in England

Write the sentence that describes each picture.

- I found a sentence describing each picture. Yes ☐ No ☐
- I used Chatterbox 12 for help. Yes ☐ No ☐

Scrambled Countries

► **Unscramble the letters to discover the names of some countries.**

1. MAEIVTN							
2. COXMIE							
3. NACIH							
4. NIIAD							
5. NAADCA							
6. YTILA							
7. ECNFRA							
8. ANGENLD							

A Day in Vietnam

- Place the postcards in order.
- Write a brief description of each postcard.

- Draw another picture about the festival in Vietnam.
- Write a brief description of your picture.

- I found the key words in Paulette and Paul's letter.
  All of them ☐ Most of them ☐ Some of them ☐ None of them ☐
- I found the letter ______________ to understand.
  Very easy ☐ Easy ☐ Difficult ☐ Very difficult ☐

Activity 3 Fun in Mexico

SB 69

- Read the text that Paulette and Paul wrote.
- Decide which pictures they should put in their souvenir album.
- Write the number of the picture in the square.

☐ ☐

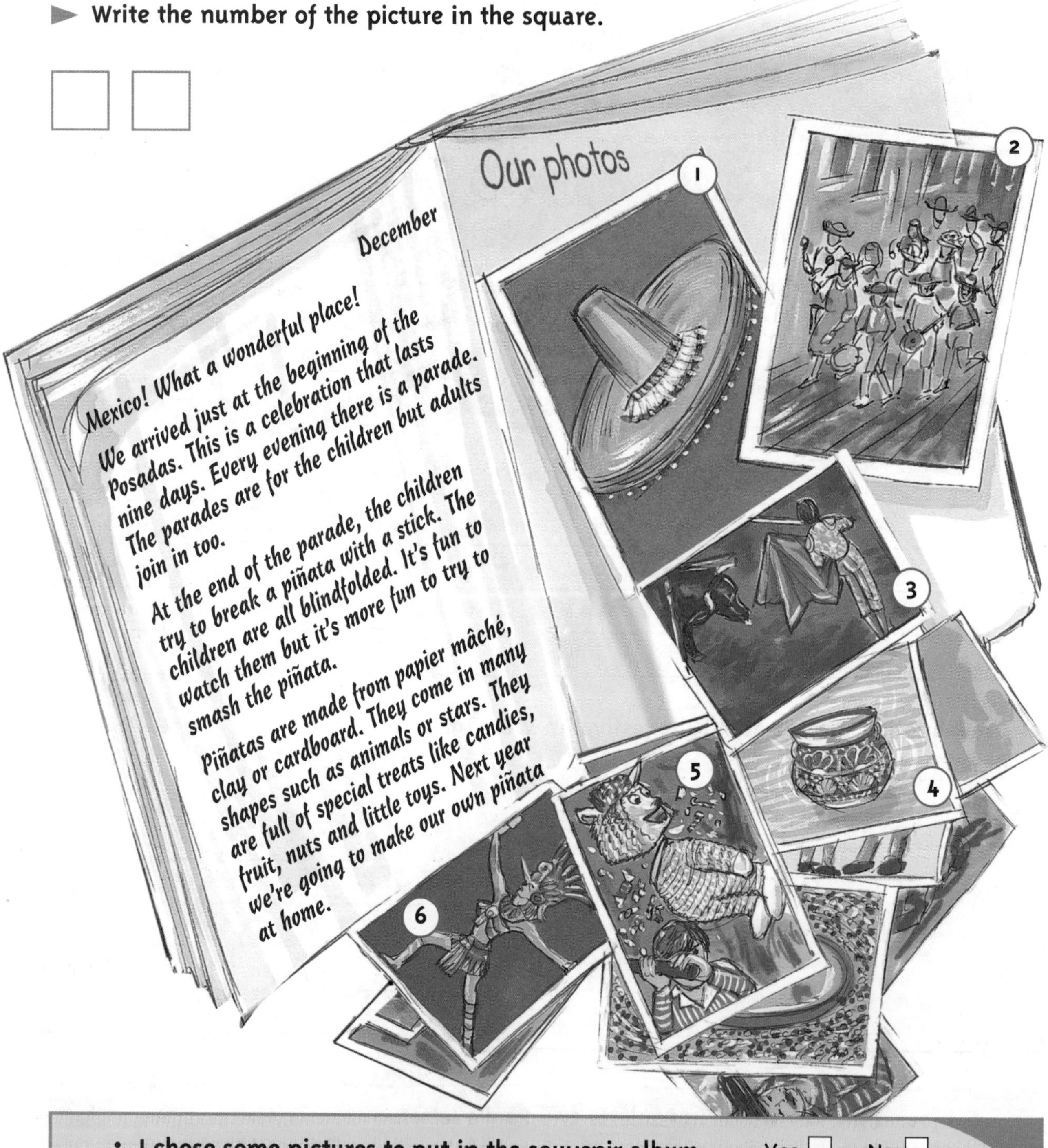

Our photos
December
Mexico! What a wonderful place!
We arrived just at the beginning of the Posadas. This is a celebration that lasts nine days. Every evening there is a parade. The parades are for the children but adults join in too.
At the end of the parade, the children try to break a piñata with a stick. The children are all blindfolded. It's fun to watch them but it's more fun to try to smash the piñata.
Piñatas are made from papier mâché, clay or cardboard. They come in many shapes such as animals or stars. They are full of special treats like candies, fruit, nuts and little toys. Next year we're going to make our own piñata at home.
1
2
3
4
5
6

- I chose some pictures to put in the souvenir album. Yes ☐ No ☐
- I found the text about Mexico ______________ to understand.
  Very easy ☐ Easy ☐ Difficult ☐ Very difficult ☐

My Piñata

► **Choose one of the recipes below and make your own piñata.**

Recipe 1. The Balloon and Paste Piñata

Materials required:
1 large balloon
newspaper
flour
water
paints
adhesive tape

Instructions:
- Blow up the balloon.
- Mix the flour and water to make a paste.
- Tear newspaper into strips.
- Cover the strips in paste.
- Cover the balloon with the newspaper strips.
- Let dry.
- Decorate.
- Cut an opening in the top of the piñata and fill with candies.
- Use adhesive tape to close the top of the piñata.

Recipe 2. The Paper Bag Piñata

Materials required:
3 large paper bags
Paint

Directions:
- Put the three bags one inside the other.
- Paint the outside with white water-based paint.
- Decorate the bag.
- Fill with candies and small toys.
- Tie the top of the bag with string.

Kwanzaa in the United Sates

SB 70

► Write your own invitation.

Come celebrate with us!

What?

When?

Who?

Why?

Where?

- I understand what Kwanzaa is about. Yes ☐ No ☐
- I wrote my own invitation with ☐ or without ☐ help.

► **Use this form to plan your scrapbook.**

► **Complete the information about your choice of festival or celebration.**

My Plan

Name of festival or celebration:

____

Country where it takes place: ______________________________

When it takes place: ______________________________

What I will put on the cover of my scrapbook: ______________________

____

____

Pictures to put in my scrapbook: ______________________________

____

Web sites I visited for information: ______________________________

____

Draft of my text: ______________________________

____

____

____

Who helped me edit my text: ______________________________

What I will put on the cover of my invitation: ______________________

____

- **I prepared a scrapbook about** ______________________________ .
- **I am satisfied with my scrapbook.**

Extremely ☐ Very ☐ Not very ☐ Not at all ☐

Invent a Celebration

- Invent a special celebration.
- Use form A as a model.
- Use form B to write your plan.

FORM A

What will the day be called? Freedom Day

What will it celebrate? The first day of summer vacation

When will it take place? June 25

What special activities will occur on this day?

Children will have a parade. They will go to the swimming pool on their bikes, skateboards or rollerblades. There will be a barbecue and fireworks at night. Everyone will wear a headband with a special symbol. Parents will give their children a summer gift, like a new swimsuit or bike helmet.

What special symbol will represent your day? A flag with a bird flying out of a cage

FORM B

What will the day be called? ______

What will it celebrate? ______

When will it take place? ______

What special activities will occur on this day?

______

______

______

______

What special symbol will represent your day? ______

Unit 9

Forever Friends

Hand in Hand

- Choose a hand gesture.
- Draw the contour of your hand gesture.

- Listen to your teacher.
- Write the information on your handprint.

- **I learned something new about my partners.**
  All of them ☐ Most of them ☐ Some of them ☐ None of them ☐
- **I used Chatterbox 10 for help.** Yes ☐ No ☐

Extension Activity

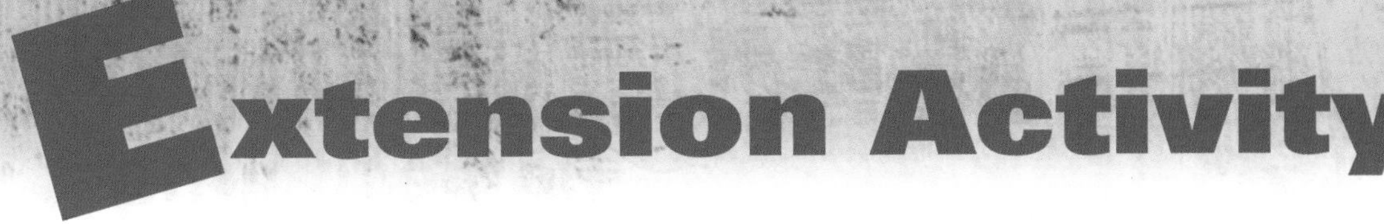

Give Us a Hand!

- **Work with your partners to invent a team handshake or signal.**
- **Draw your handshake or signal.**

My partners are:

___

___

___

Our handshake or signal is:

The Homecoming

SB 75-77

► **Put the events in order.**

☐ The friends decorate the house and wait for Henry's wife to return.

☐ Lori meets Old Man Pettigrew and sees a photograph of his wife.

☐ Lori learns that Mrs Pettigrew is dead and that the friends pretend she is coming home.

☐ Meg comes to visit Mr Pettigrew and he tells her about the letter he received.

☐ Joe and Henry plan a welcome-home party for Henry's wife.

► **Write each sentence in the appropriate box.**

First, ______________________________

____

↓

Next, ______________________________

____

↓

Then, ______________________________

____

↓

After that, ______________________________

____

↓

Finally, ______________________________

____

- **I enjoyed the play *The Homecoming*.** Yes ☐ No ☐
- **I thought the text was:**
  Very easy ☐ Easy ☐ Difficult ☐ Very difficult ☐

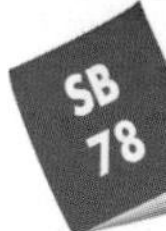

Activity 2 Quite a Character!

SB 78

- Choose one character from the play.
- Describe that character.

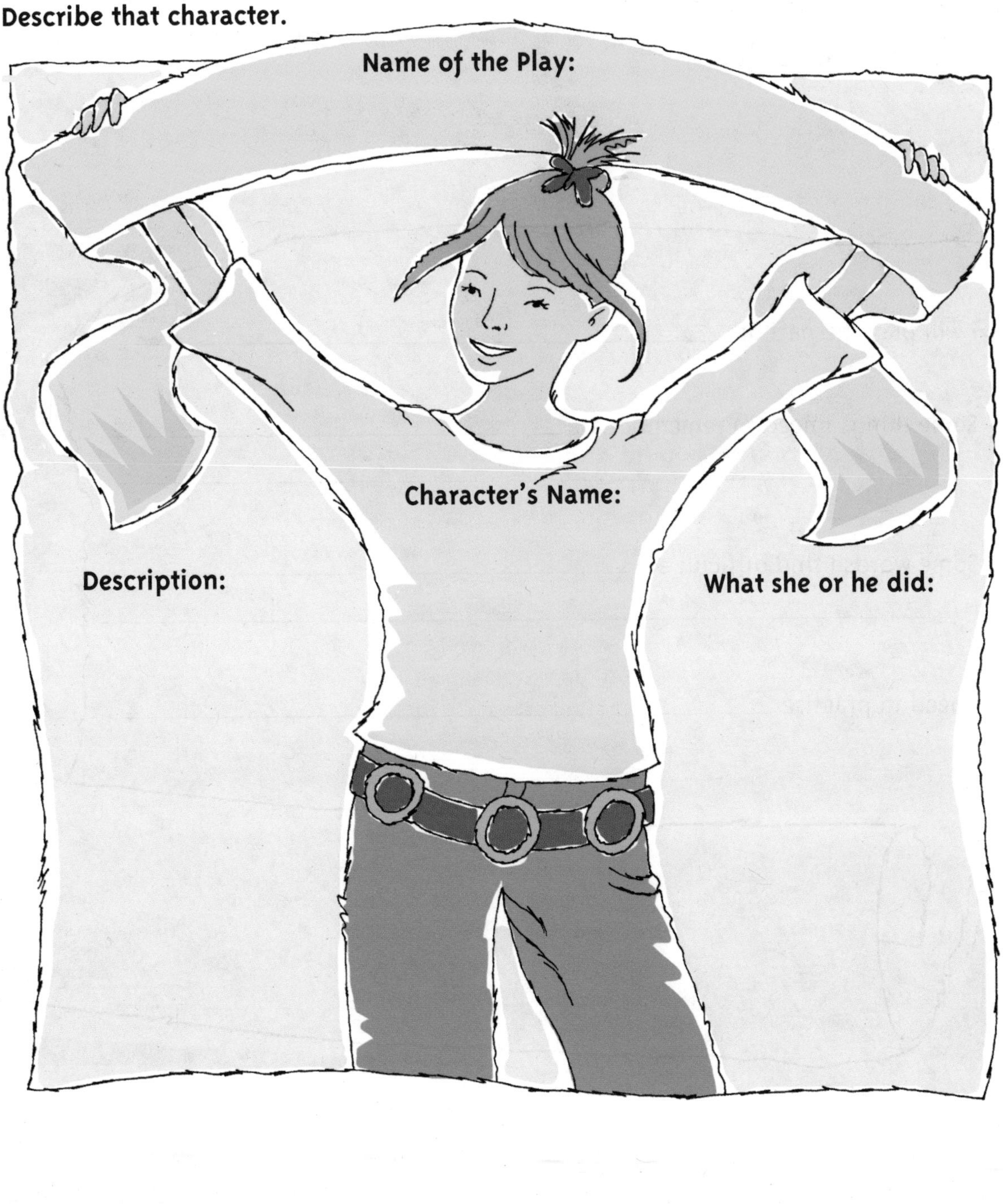
Name of the Play:
Character's Name:
Description:
What she or he did:

- I described this character in the play: ______________________ .
- I spoke English with my partners.
  Always ☐ Most of the time ☐ Some of the time ☐ Never ☐

Activity 3 Made for the Role

SB 79

- Study your lines.
- Practise your part.
- Complete the sentences.

I will play the part of ______________________.

Some things I need to remember are ______________________
______________________.

Some words I find difficult are ______________________
____

I need to practise ______________________.

- **When I practised my part, I worked:**
  Very hard ☐ Moderately hard ☐ Not very hard ☐ Not hard at all ☐
- **I used Chatterbox 1 for help.** Yes ☐ No ☐

Opening Night

► Design a program for your performance.

► Write the information for your program.

____

Characters:

____
____
____
____
____
____

Performance:

Date: ______________________________

Time: ______________________________

Place: ______________________________

Cast of Characters:

____
____
____
____
____
____
____
____
____
____
____
____

- I used Chatterbox 8 for help. Yes ☐ No ☐
- I helped my partners design a program for our performance. Yes ☐ No ☐

Plan your performance of the play *The Homecoming*.

Choose the format for your performance.

____

We will have music. Yes ☐ No ☐

We will use props. Yes ☐ No ☐

The props we need are ______________________________

______________________________.

We will have costumes. Yes ☐ No ☐

We will bring ______________________________

______________________________.

- **During this unit, I worked:**
  Very hard ☐ Moderately hard ☐ Not very hard ☐ Not hard at all ☐

Extension Activity

My Review

► **Write a review of *The Homecoming*.**

Mystery Word

- Find the words in the puzzle.
- Then find the mystery word.

N	C	G	M	A	R	G	O	R	P
A	H	N	E	P	A	R	T	I	E
R	A	I	P	O	R	P	H	S	R
R	R	T	L	T	I	S	I	E	F
A	A	T	A	R	D	T	C	N	O
T	C	E	C	N	C	A	T	I	R
O	T	S	E	A	S	G	I	L	M
R	E	I	R	T	G	E	R	E	A
W	R	P	N	I	A	T	R	U	C
F	A	U	D	I	E	N	C	E	T

ACT
AUDIENCE
CAST
CHARACTER
CURTAIN
FRIENDSHIP
LINES
NARRATOR
PART
PERFORM
PLACE
PRACTISE
PROGRAM
PROP
SCRIPT
SETTING
STAGE

Mystery word: P _ _ _ _ _ _ _ _ _

Who am I? ____________________

Unit 10

Signs of the Times

Yesterday and Tomorrow

- Describe what you see.
- Use this page for your notes.

- I found ______________ different signs on the cover page.
- I described the pictures during the warm-up activity. Yes ☐ No ☐

Fashion Signs

SB 85

- Describe today's fashions.
- Draw or paste pictures of these fashions.

Today's Fashions

Headgear		Footwear
Coats and jackets		Pants and skirts

- **The texts were ______________ to read.**
  Very easy ☐ Easy ☐ Difficult ☐ Very difficult ☐
- **I am happy with my fashion page.** Yes ☐ No ☐

Extension Activity

In Fashion

- Look at the topics below.
- Find illustrations of this year's models from magazines, catalogues or flyers.
- Glue your favourites on the page.

In the year ______

Bicycles

Cars

Computers

Toys

Games

Signs and Sounds

Read the reviews and answer the questions.

What are the names of the two groups?

______________________ ______________________

Which eras do they represent?

______________________ ______________________

Why are these groups popular with young people?

______________________ ______________________

______________________ ______________________

______________________ ______________________

______________________ ______________________

Which group would you like to hear? Why?

____

____

____

____

Which group(s) of today do you like? Why?

____

____

____

____

- **I answered the questions about the music groups on the handout.**
  All of them ☐ Most of them ☐ Some of them ☐ None of them ☐
- **I used Chatterbox 8 for help.** Yes ☐ No ☐

Sign Up for Fun

- Listen to the conversations.
- List the activities mentioned.

PAST • PAST • PAST • PAST • PAST • PAST • PAST • PAST • PAST

____

____

____

____

____

FUTURE • FUTURE • FUTURE • FUTURE • FUTURE • FUTURE

____

____

____

____

____

- I was able to name ________ activities.
- The conversations on the recording were ____________ to understand.
  Very easy ☐ Easy ☐ Difficult ☐ Very difficult ☐

Signs of Technology

► **Read the magazine articles and complete the charts.**

Features: ______________________

____

Users: ______________________

____

Operation: ______________________

____

Features: ______________________

____

Users: ______________________

____

Operation: ______________________

____

Features: ______________________

____

Users: ______________________

____

Operation: ______________________

____

- **I spoke English with my partner.**
  Always ☐ Most of the time ☐ Some of the time ☐ Never ☐
- **I wrote down information about the three types of telephones.** Yes ☐ No ☐

Use this questionnaire to plan your presentation.

- What four categories will there be on our sign?

____

- Who will present each part?

Category: ____ Presenter: ____	Category: ____ Presenter: ____
Category: ____ Presenter: ____	Category: ____ Presenter: ____

- What Web sites can we visit for information? What keywords can we use?

____

____

- What pictures should we look for?

____

____

- What kind of audio or video material can we use?

____

- What other material do we need?

____

- Who will bring what?

____

____

- **During the wrap-up, I worked:**
  Extremely hard ☐ Very hard ☐ Not very hard ☐ Not hard at all ☐

Extra Activity

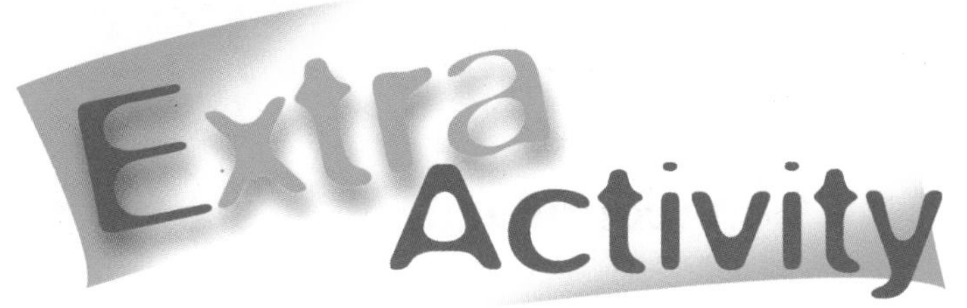

My Sign

- Create your personal sign.
- Choose one of these designs: a licence plate, a key ring, a bookplate or a sign for your bedroom door.

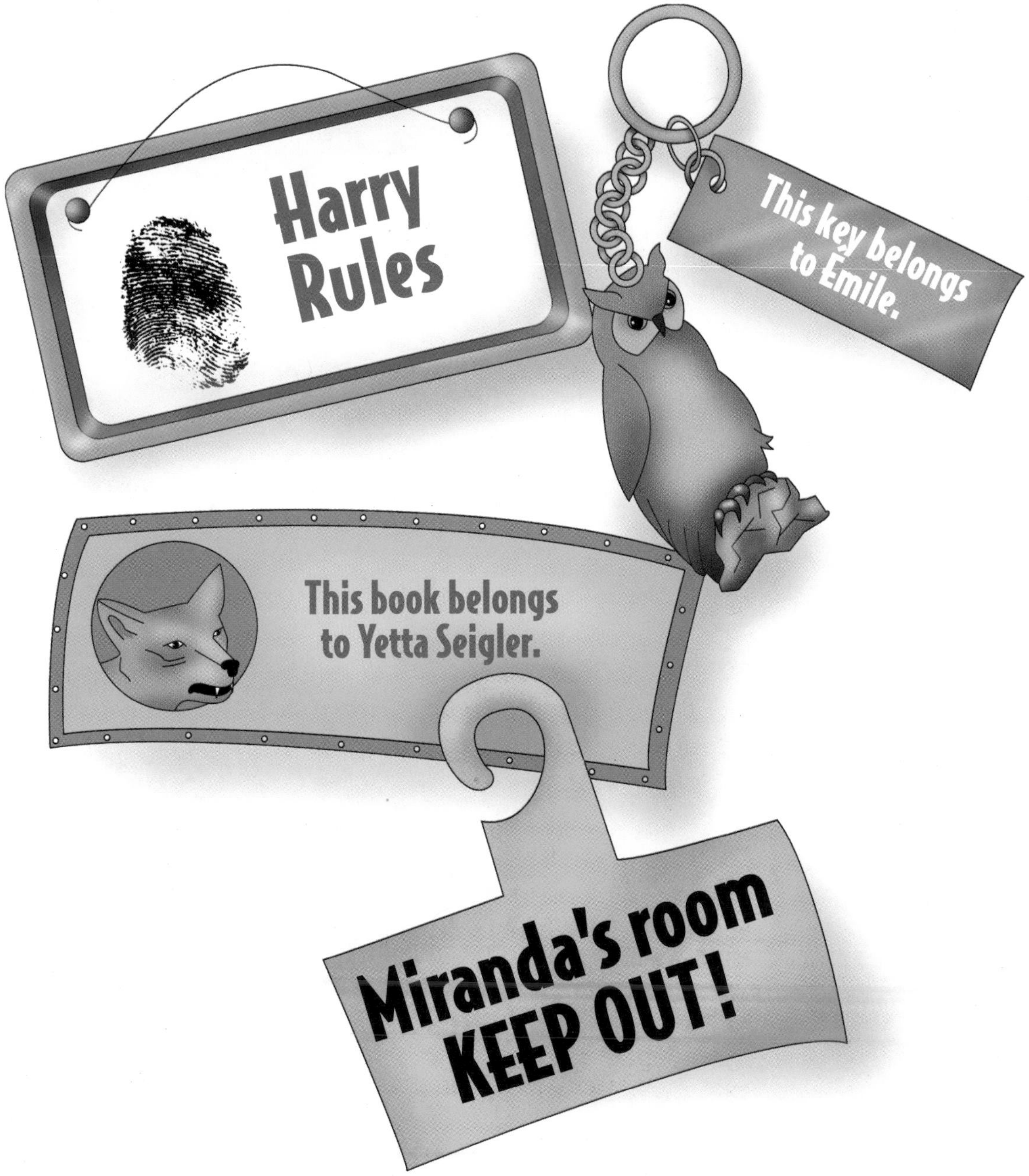
Harry Rules
This key belongs to Émile.
This book belongs to Yetta Seigler.
Miranda's room KEEP OUT!

Continued on next page

My Sign (continued)

► **Use this space to plan your design and write your text.**

Unit 11

The Forgetting Stone

A Story for Everyone

- Place each book in the appropriate category.
- Say what kind of story you prefer.

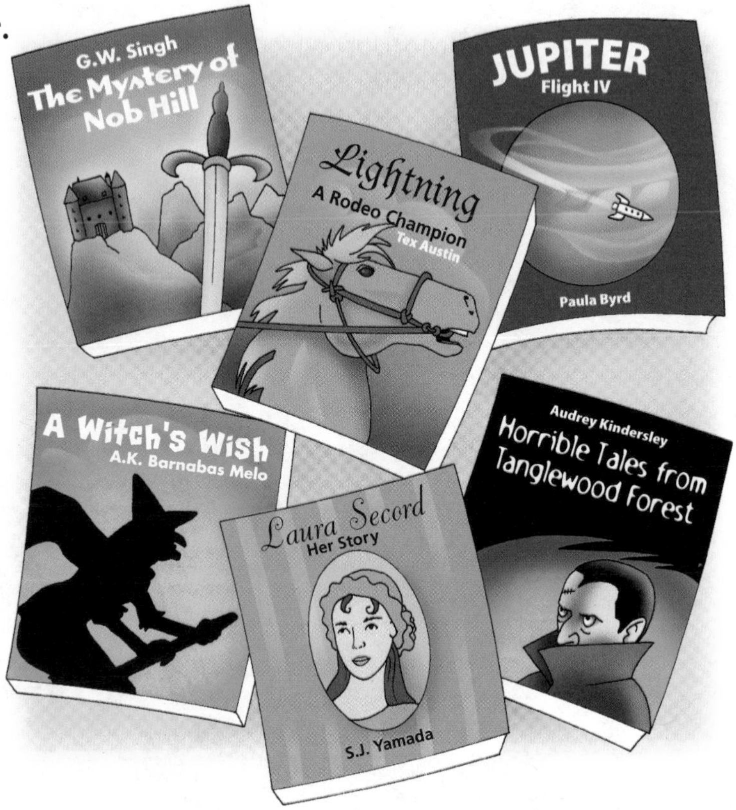

Science fiction

Biography

Mystery

Adventure

Fantasy

Horror

G.W. Singh
The Mystery of Nob Hill

JUPITER
Flight IV
Paula Byrd

Lightning
A Rodeo Champion
Tex Austin

A Witch's Wish
A.K. Barnabas Melo

Audrey Kindersley
Horrible Tales from Tanglewood Forest

Laura Secord
Her Story
S.J. Yamada

My favourite type of story is: ______________________________

- I identified the different types of stories shown on the book covers.
  All of them ☐ Most of them ☐ Some of them ☐ None of them ☐
- I used correct capitalization when I wrote the titles. Yes ☐ No ☐

Extension Activity

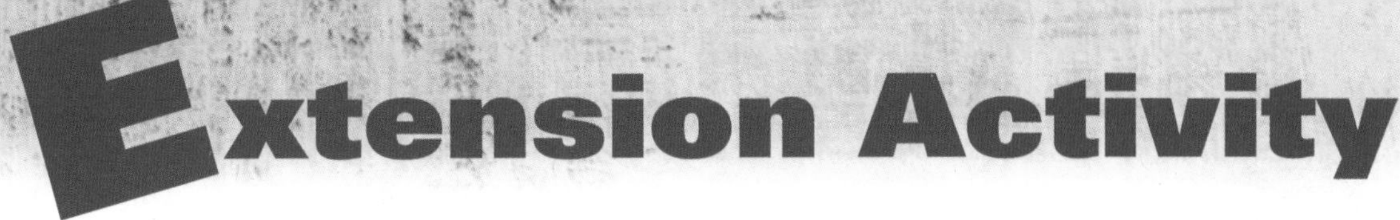

My Bookmark

► **Make a bookmark that shows the kind of story you prefer.**

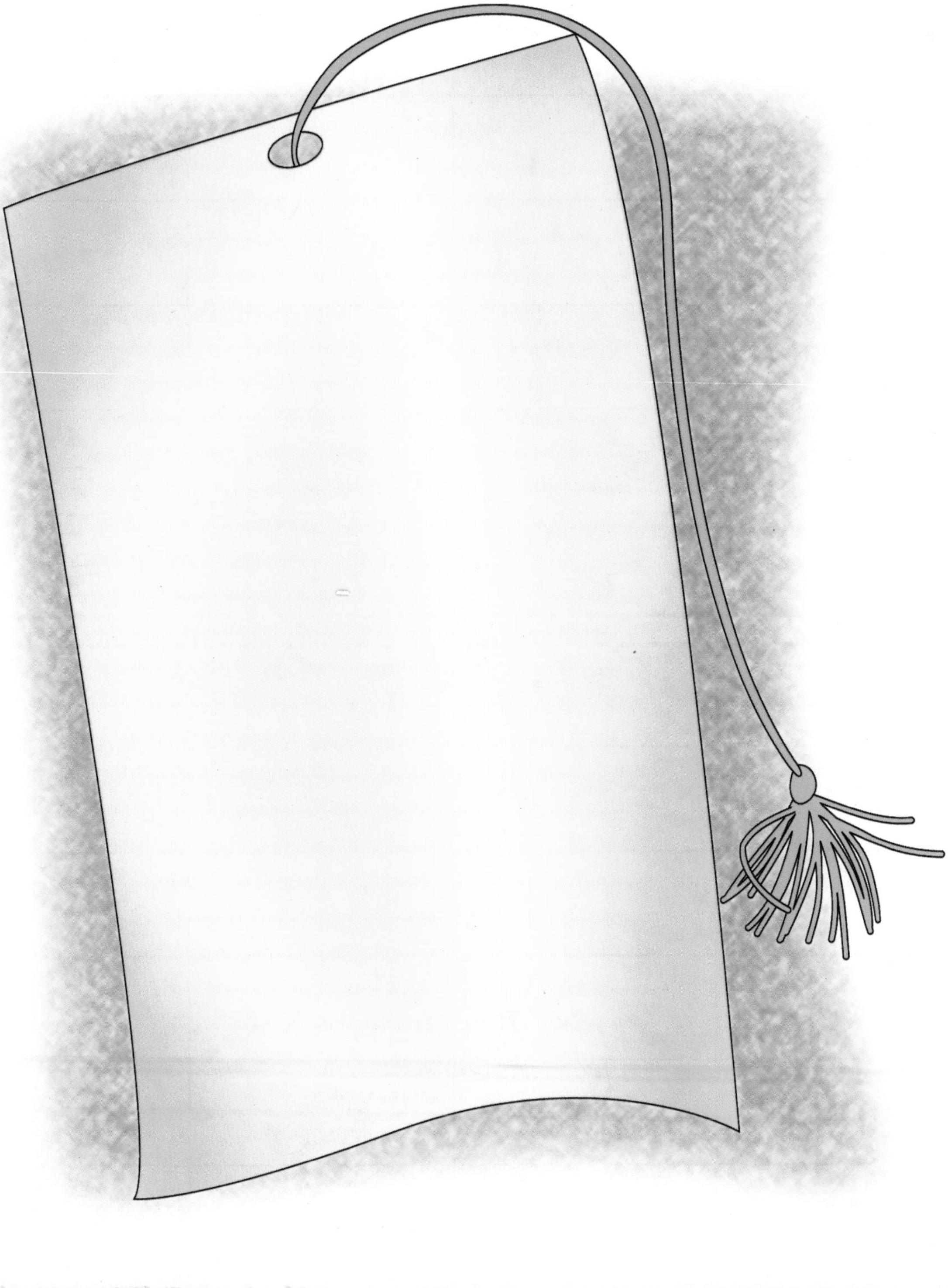

Summer Reading Chart

► **Keep a chart of the books you read during your summer vacation.**

Date:			
Title:			
Author:			
Type of story:			
Thumbs up:			
Thumbs down:			

Date:			
Title:			
Author:			
Type of story:			
Thumbs up:			
Thumbs down:			

Georgia's Discovery

Answer the questions.

1. What does Georgia like and dislike?

   ____

2. What does she hate?

   ____

3. What does she hope for?

   ____

4. Who is the man in the picture?

   ____

5. What did Georgia step on?

   ____

Check off the correct sentence on each stepping stone.

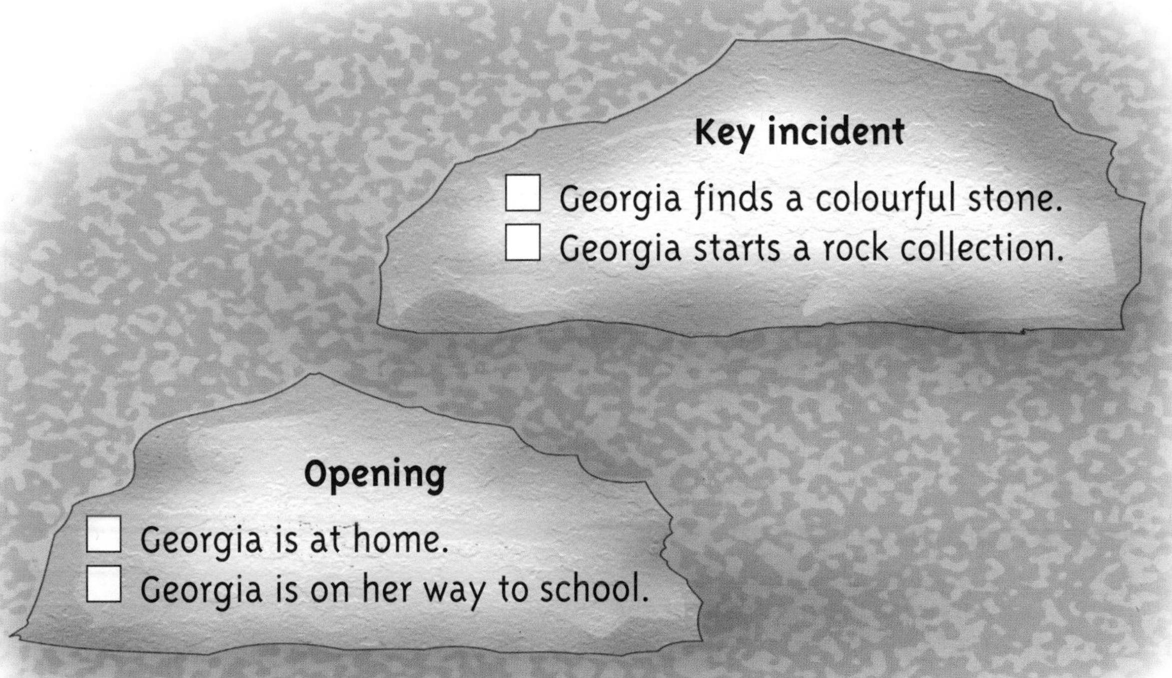

Continued on next page

Activity 1 Georgia's Discovery (continued)

► **Complete the chart with information about Georgia and yourself.**

Georgia	Me
likes . . .	I like . . .
dislikes . . .	I dislike . . .
hates . . .	I hate . . .
wants . . .	I want . . .

- **I understood the first part of the story.**
  All of it ☐ Most of it ☐ Some of it ☐ None of it ☐
- **I am like ☐ unlike ☐ Georgia because** ______________________________
  ____.

Lost for Words

Answer the questions.

1. How does Georgia feel when she touches the stone.

___

2. What is wrong with the teacher?

___

3. What is wrong with Ms Vedden?

___

4. What does Georgia's mother do?

___

5. How does Georgia feel?

___

6. What do you think *krowfosdrow* means?

___

Check off the correct sentence on the stepping stone.

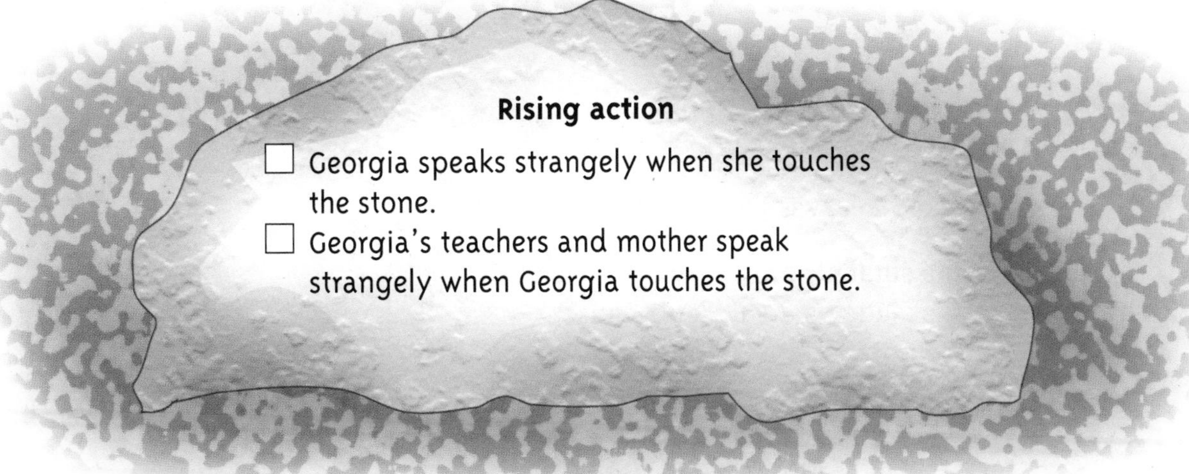

Rising action

- ☐ Georgia speaks strangely when she touches the stone.
- ☐ Georgia's teachers and mother speak strangely when Georgia touches the stone.

- **I think this part of the story is funny ☐ strange ☐ interesting ☐.**

Trouble for Georgia

Answer the questions.

1. How do the parents feel?

____

2. How do the students feel?

____

3. What does Georgia realize?

____

4. What does she want to do now?

____

Check off the correct sentences on the stepping stones.

Climax

☐ Georgia decides to write everything down.
☐ Georgia decides to throw away the stone.

Rising action

☐ Georgia tests the rock.
☐ Georgia leaves the rock at home.

☐ The students are angry with Georgia.
☐ The students are upset because their grades are falling.

- **My prediction was correct.** Yes ☐ No ☐
- **I worked well with my partner.** Yes ☐ No ☐

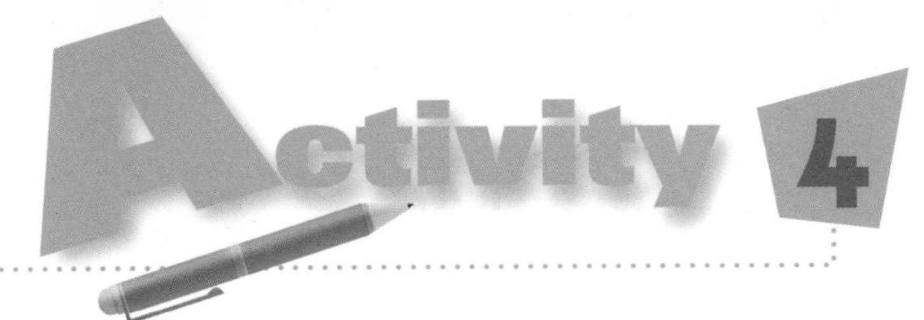

Activity 4 Well Done, Georgia!

SB 100

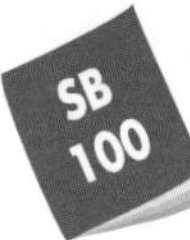

Answer the questions.

1. What does Mr Renzo say to Georgia?

____

2. What does the word *krowfosdrow* mean?

____

3. How did Georgia think of the story?

____

Check off the correct sentence on the stepping stone.

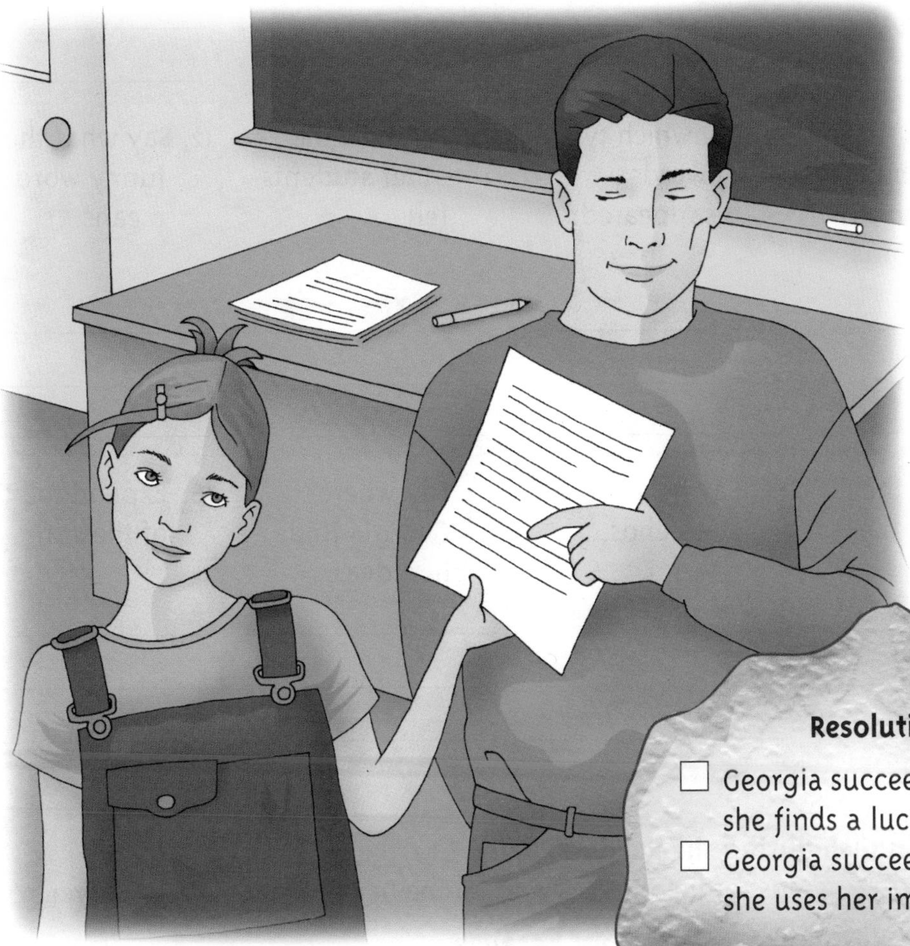

Resolution

- ☐ Georgia succeeds because she finds a lucky stone.
- ☐ Georgia succeeds because she uses her imagination.

Continued on next page

Activity 4 Well Done, Georgia! (continued)

Readers' Rally

▶ **Find someone who can . . .**

1. Name one thing that Georgia likes. ________ ________ ________	2. Name one thing that Georgia dislikes. ________ ________ ________	3. Name one thing that Georgia hates. ________ ________ ________	4. Repeat what Georgia wanted the teacher to say. ________ ________ ________
5. Say what Georgia collects. ________ ________ ________	6. Describe the stone Georgia found. ________ ________ ________	7. Say the funny word from the story. ________ ________ ________	8. Say how the stone made Georgia feel. ________ ________ ________
9. Name the three people who forgot how to say certain words. ________ ________ ________	10. Say which type of words disappeared. ________ ________ ________	11. Say how the other students felt. ________ ________ ________	12. Say what the funny word means. ________ ________ ________
13. Say what the climax of the story is. ________ ________ ________	14. Say how the story ends. ________ ________ ________	15. Say where Georgia finds her ideas. ________ ________ ________	16. Explain the title of the story. ________ ________ ________

- **I spoke English during the Readers' Rally.**
  Always ☐ Most of the time ☐ Some of the time ☐ Never ☐
- **I liked** ☐ **didn't like** ☐ **this story because** ____________________
  ____.

Story Map

► **Complete the stepping stones for Georgia's story.**

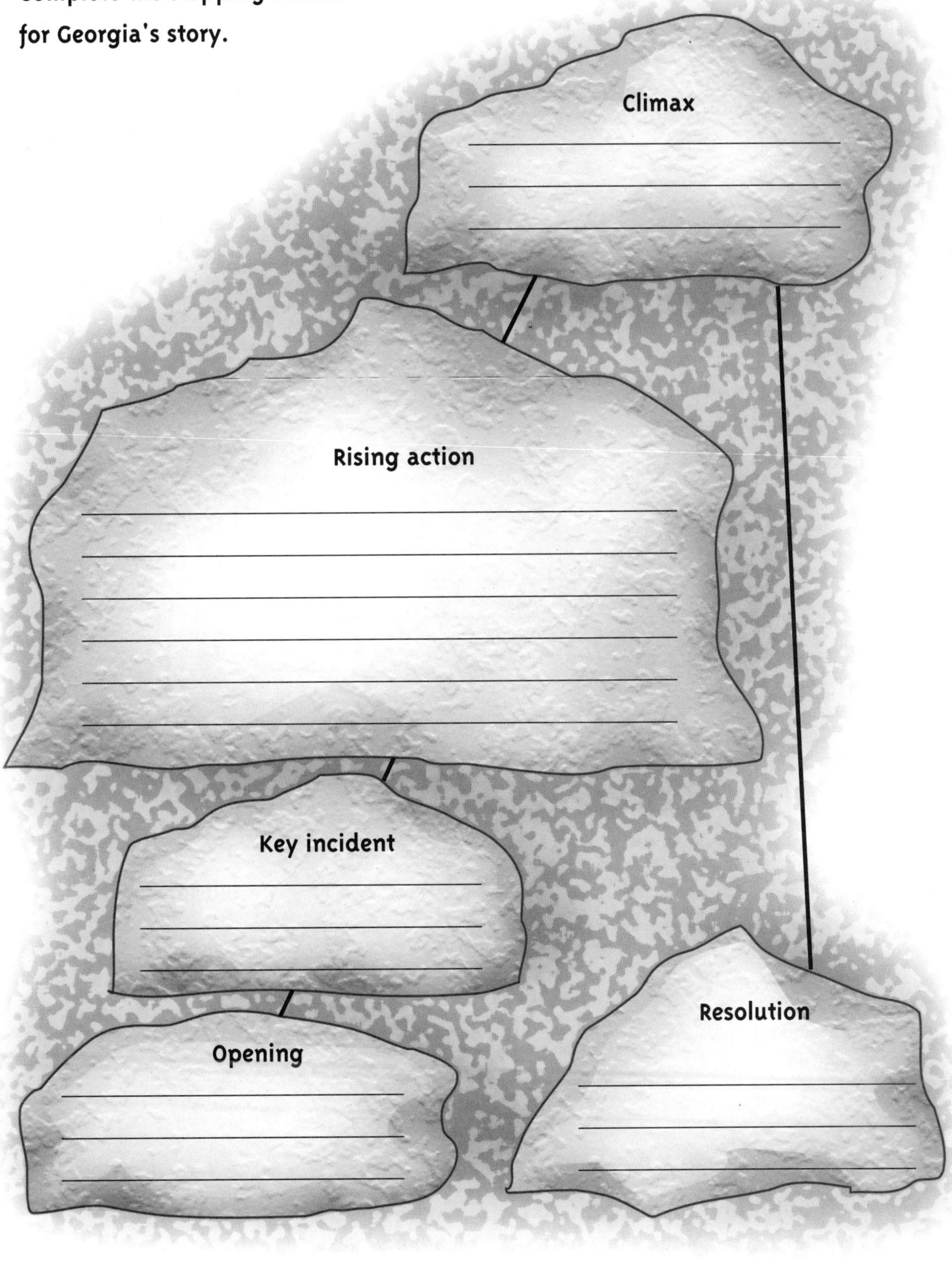

Climax

____

____

____

Rising action

____

____

____

____

____

____

Key incident

____

____

____

Opening

____

____

____

Resolution

____

____

____

Continued on next page

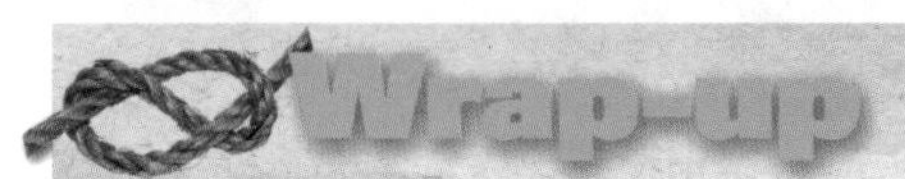

Wrap-up (continued)

My Story

► **Complete the stepping stones for your story.**

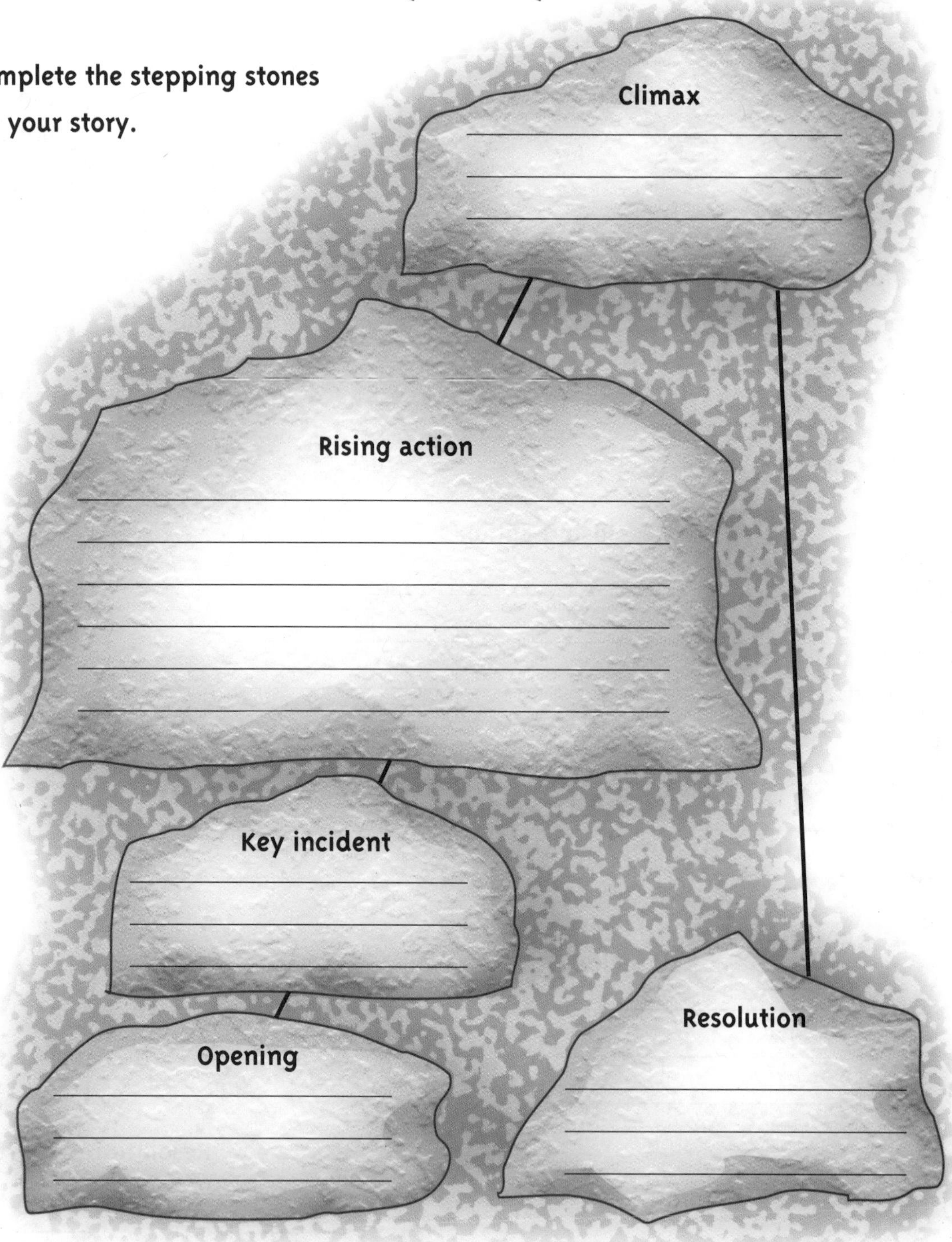
Climax
Rising action
Key incident
Opening
Resolution

- **I made a story map for my own story.** Yes ☐ No ☐
- **During this unit, I worked:**
  Very hard ☐ Moderately hard ☐ Not very hard ☐ Not hard at all ☐

Extension Activity

A Story of My Own

► Use your story map to write and illustrate your own story.

And the Winner Is . . .

► Survey your classmates to discover which type of story is the most popular.

Name	Science Fiction	Biography	Mystery	Adventure	Fantasy	Horror
Totals						

The most popular type of story is ______________________________.

Unit 12

The Welcome Wall

▶ Write the unit numbers and titles.

▶ Match each statement with its unit.

	Unit ____. ________________ ________________	I discovered the meaning of friendship. ________
	Unit ____. ________________ ________________	I compared toys from the present and the past. ________
	Unit ____. ________________ ________________	I learned about some acts of courage. ________
	Unit ____. ________________ ________________	I reviewed what I studied in this book. ________
	Unit ____. ________________ ________________	I discovered what some names mean. ________
	Unit ____. ________________ ________________	I discovered what some people are afraid of. ________
	Unit ____. ________________ ________________	I participated in a record-breaking event. ________
	Unit ____. ________________ ________________	I discovered some tools I can use when learning English. ________
	Unit ____. ________________ ________________	I found out about my special day. ________
	Unit ____. ________________ ________________	I learned about some special celebrations around the world. ________
	Unit ____. ________________ ________________	I learned that imagination is a powerful tool. ________
	Unit ____. ________________ ________________	I learned about the past, the present and the future. ________

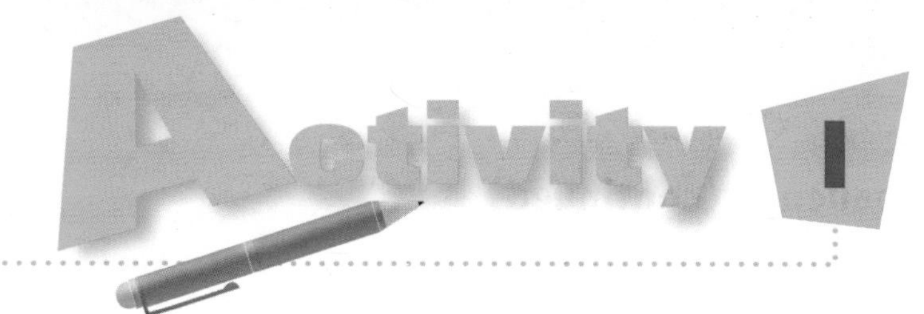

Activity 1 Chatterbox Challenge

SB 105

Fill in the form as you find the matching titles and activities.

Unit	Wrap-up Activity
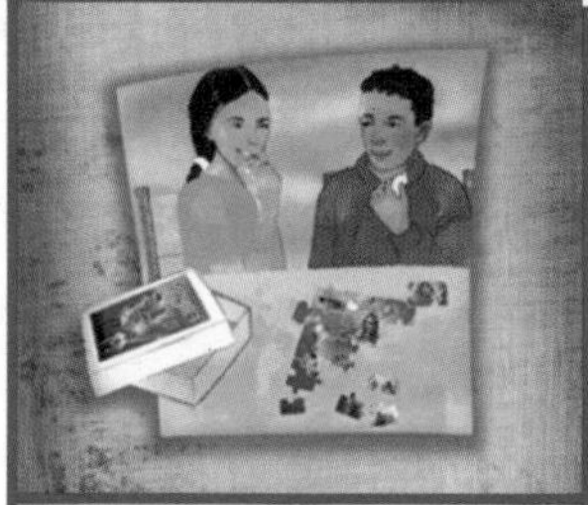	
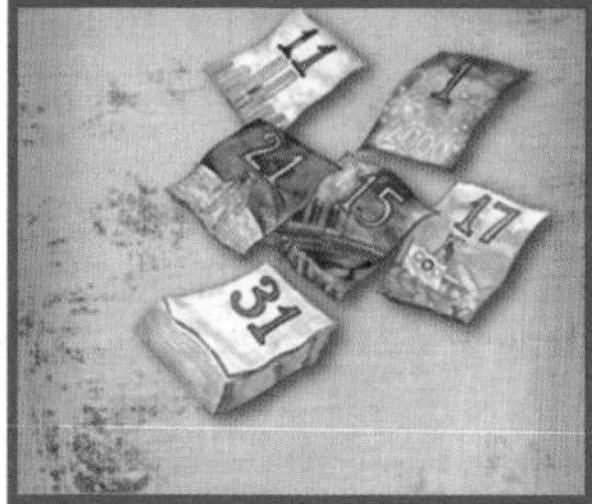	
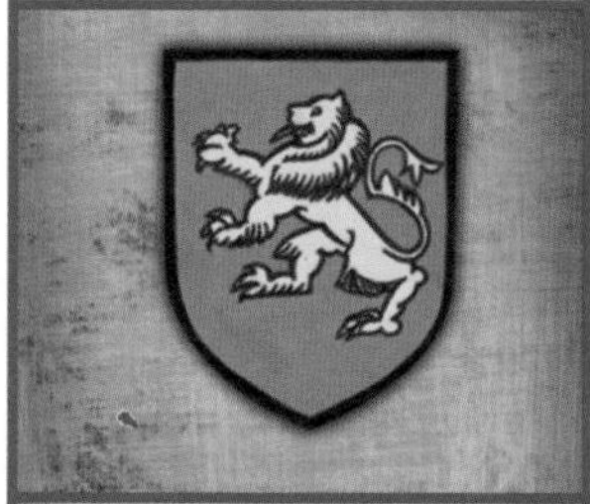	
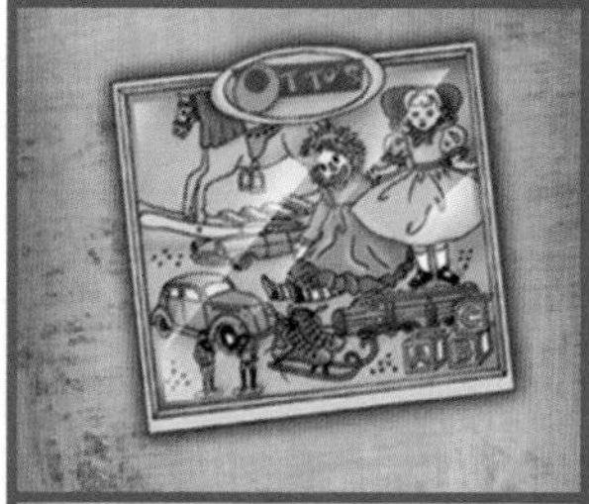	
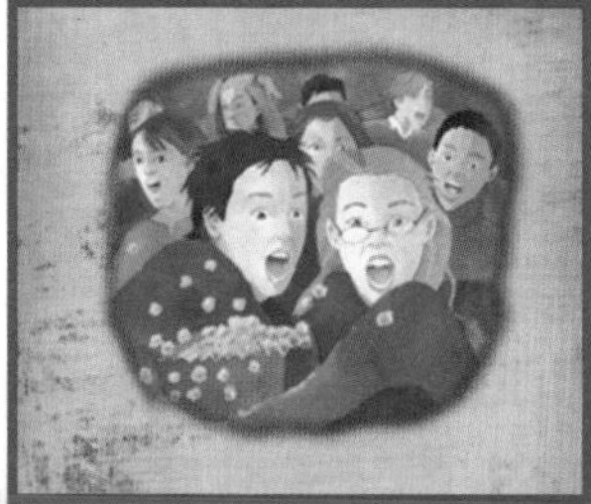	
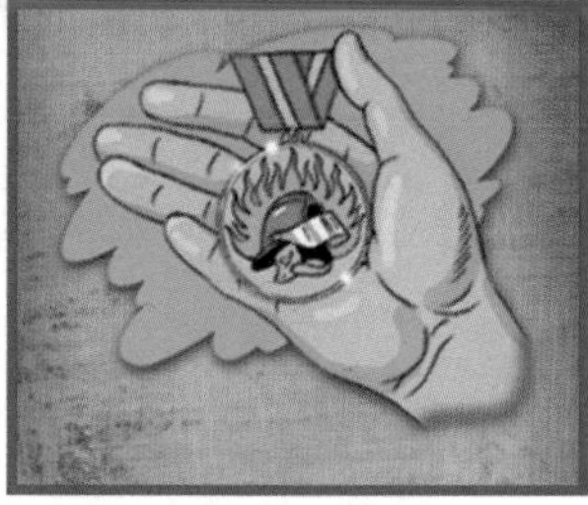	

Continued on next page

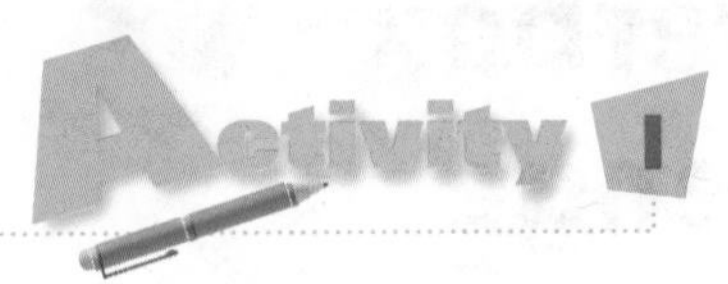

Activity 1 Chatterbox Challenge (continued)

Unit	Wrap-up Activity
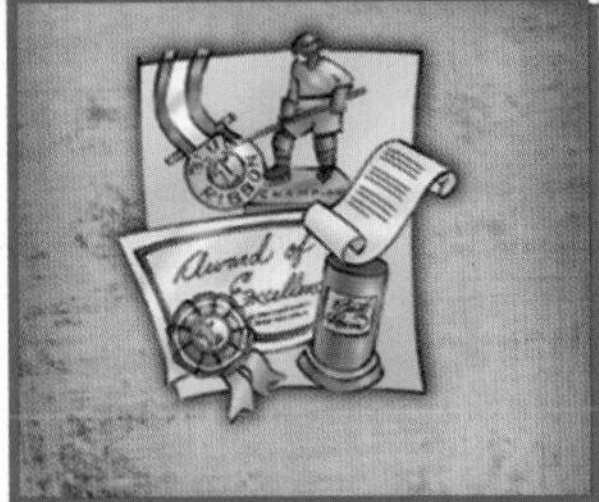	
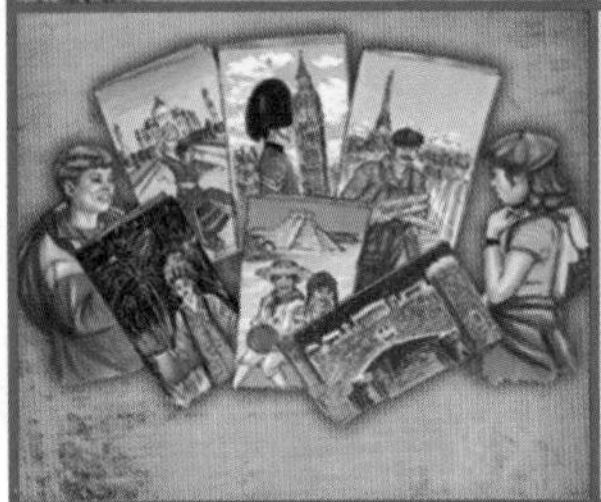	
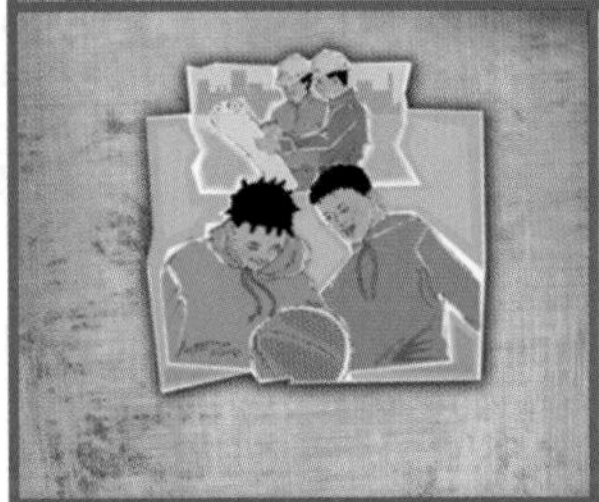	
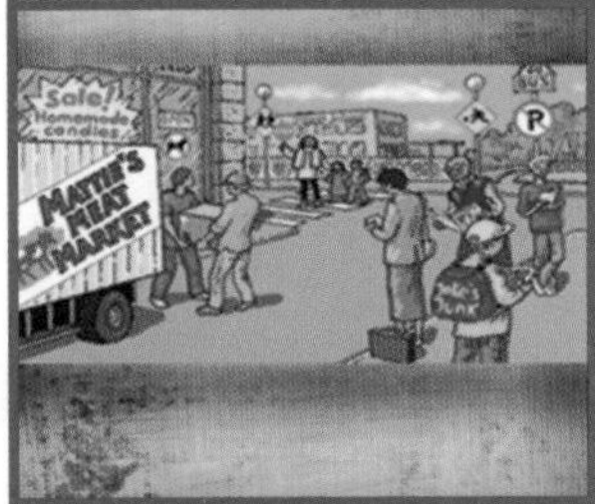	
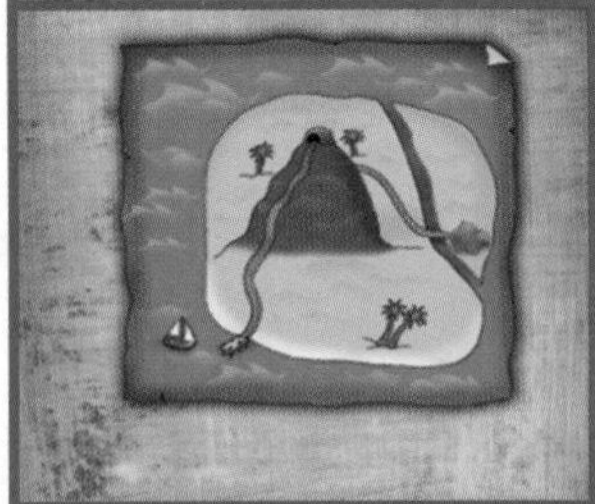	
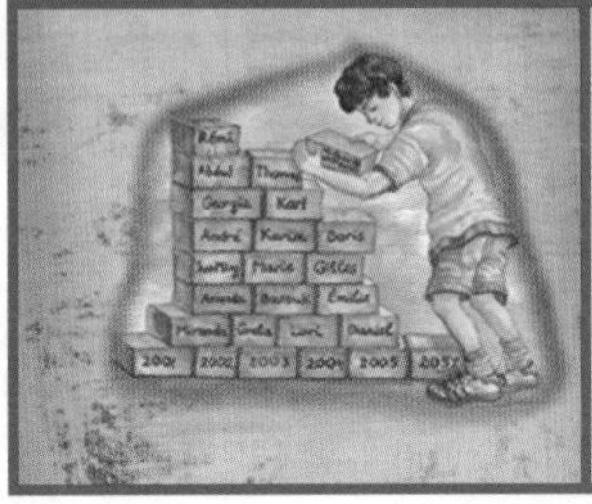	

The Reader's Review

Write the number of the summary beside the title of the story.

1. Take this advice: Don't look back!

2. In this story, the peasant is the noble one.

3. Imagination is a powerful tool.

4. A young girl learns the meaning of friendship.

Forever Friends ______

Down Under ______

The Keeper ______

The Forgetting Stone ______

Extension Activity

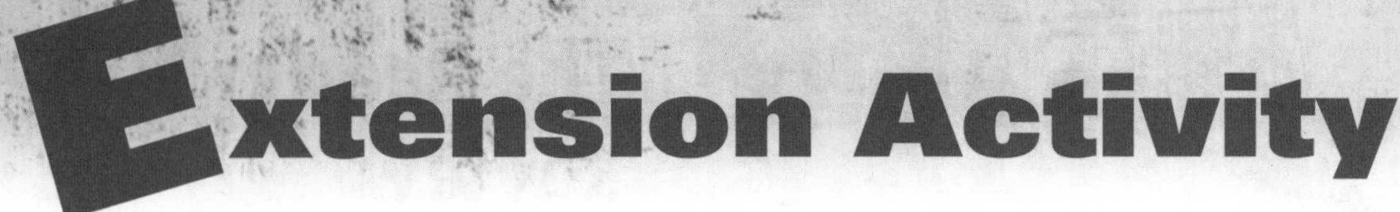

Our Story Markers

- Use one of the models to create a special way to remember your favourite Chatterbox story.
- Trace or photocopy the model and decorate your choice.

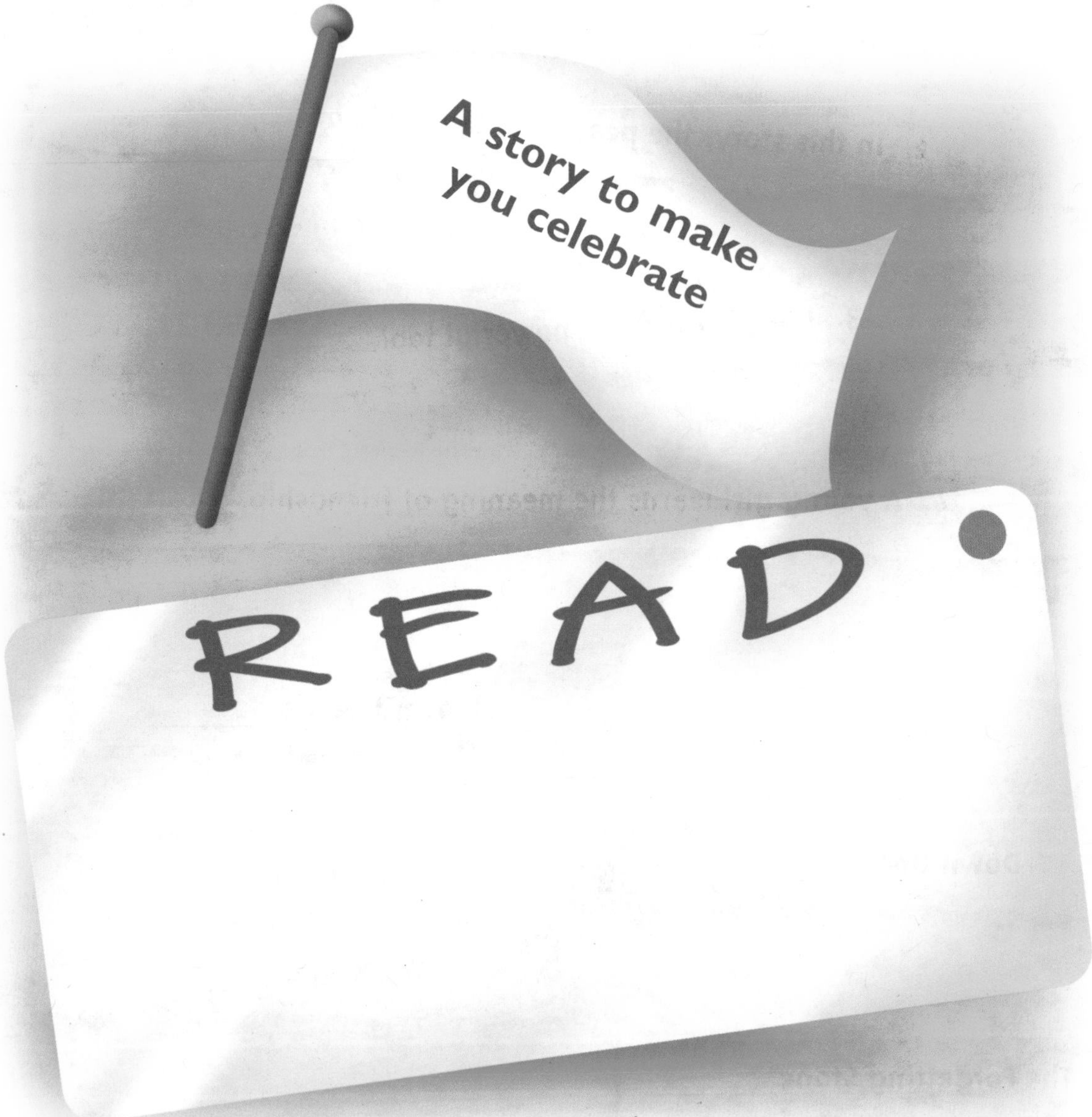
A story to make you celebrate
READ

Continued on next page

Extension Activity (continued)

Activity 3 Tools for Tomorrow

Use this page to list all the strategies you and your partner mention.

Me	My partner

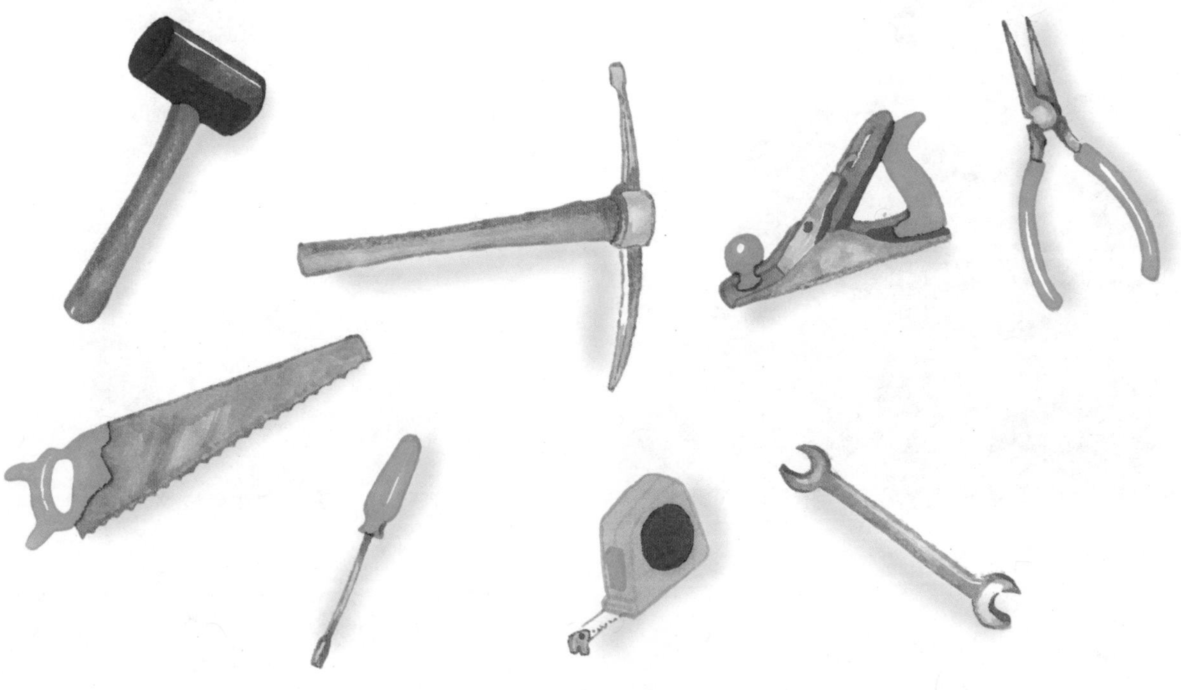

Super Cool!

Place each unit in one of the categories.

	Super cool!	Cool!	Boring!

Unit 1. Learning Tools

Unit 2. On This Day

Unit 3. Words of Honour

Unit 4. Playing Around

Unit 5. Fear Files

Unit 6. It Takes Courage

Unit 7. Beat the Record

Unit 8. Celebrating the World

Unit 9. Forever Friends

Unit 10. Signs of the Times

Unit 11. The Forgetting Stone

Wrap-up

SB 109

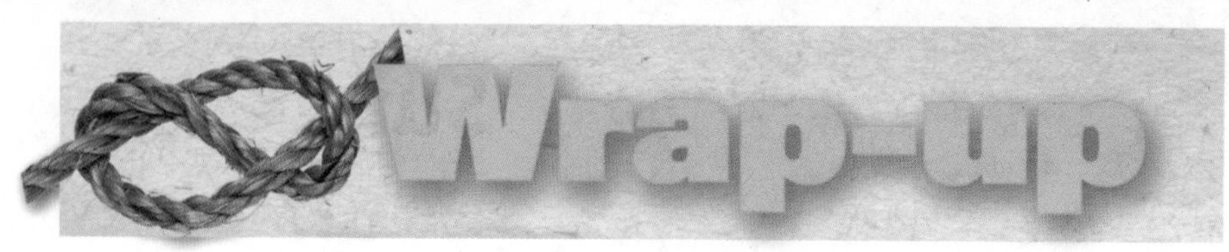

Complete the brick as you work through the unit.

My favourite unit is: ____________________

My favourite wrap-up activity is: ____________________

My favourite story is: ____________________

My advice is: ____________________

Word Quiz

- Find out how many words you have learned.
- Put a check next to each word you know and a ? next to those you are not certain of.
- Do this as quickly as you can.

	sportswear ☐	ugly ☐	clay ☐
crowbar ☐	darkness ☐	dock ☐	
	cast ☐	audience ☐	pretend ☐
forever ☐	greet ☐	device ☐	
	candy cane ☐	proud ☐	blink ☐
butterfly ☐	bathe ☐	reach ☐	
	freedom ☐	level ☐	wallpaper ☐
available ☐	cheer ☐	lyrics ☐	
	lines ☐	key incident ☐	movable ☐
award ☐	closet ☐	challenge ☐	
	homecoming ☐	laugh at ☐	blindfolded ☐

Continued on next page

Word Quiz (continued)

	play ☐	harmful ☐	evil ☐
opening ☐	allow ☐	curtain ☐	
	embarrassed ☐	electric sander ☐	hammer ☐
diary ☐	carpenter's square ☐	heartbroken ☐	
hop ☐	garbage ☐	phone booth ☐	ghost ☐
mallet ☐	flag ☐	electric drill ☐	
	full-length ☐	beat ☐	lonely ☐
electric saw ☐	pickaxe ☐	crowded ☐	
	fierce ☐	cardboard ☐	axe ☐
ferocious ☐	headlight ☐	performance ☐	kid ☐
	push button ☐	lawn mower ☐	elevator ☐

Continued on next page

Word Quiz (continued)

	washable ☐	whisper ☐	tough ☐
skunk ☐	hate ☐	thunderstorm ☐	
	tear ☐	resolution ☐	shelter ☐
hit ☐	smash ☐	sibling ☐	
	home ☐	track ☐	stuffed ☐
tape measure ☐	jump ☐	trick ☐	
saw ☐	rocking chair ☐	rough ☐	upset ☐
hover ☐	screwdriver ☐	helmet ☐	ye ☐
	shiver ☐	lean ☐	scrapbook ☐
please ☐	lovable ☐	wedding ☐	
	climax ☐	scream ☐	strength ☐

Continued on next page

Word Quiz (continued)

treat ☐	lullaby ☐	heavy-duty ☐	
struggle ☐	unbreakable ☐	perspire ☐	
rotary dial ☐	scared ☐	stage ☐	
script ☐	pit ☐	shake ☐	
sweat ☐	smooth ☐	wisdom ☐	
removable ☐	whistle ☐	reckless ☐	
wrench ☐	snake ☐	pliers ☐	
wolf ☐	plane ☐	shield ☐	
rising action ☐	plot ☐	wonder ☐	
prop ☐	tiny ☐	timeless ☐	
sleigh ☐	shore ☐	steady ☐	

Memory Wall

► **Ask your friends and teachers to write farewell messages to you.**